SLAYING

DODGING DOUGHNUTS

One mum's fight to save her daughter from anorexia

EMMA CARTER

First edition printed in the United Kingdom 2023.

A CIP catalogue record of this book is available from the British Library.

ISBN (Paperback):   978-1-3999-4530-1
ISBN (Hardcover):   978-1-3999-4544-8
Imprint: Independently published
Editor: Christine Beech
Cover design: Jenn Garside Illustration and Graphic Design
Typesetting: Matthew J Bird

For further information about this book, please contact the author at:
emmacarterwriter@gmail.com

I dedicate this book to my incredible daughter, Poppy, who amazes me with her strength and resilience.

Also, to my amazing son, Jordan, who has been a great support and his hugs have been a lifesaver to me.

I'm so grateful to have both of you in my life and I love you to the moon and back.

If you want something in life, go and fight for it.

Don't give up. Keep believing in yourself and make it happen.

Foreword

My name is Marg Oaten and I am married to Dennis. We have 4 children and 7 amazing grandchildren.

In 1994, at just 10 years of age, our precious daughter was diagnosed with the eating disorder Anorexia Nervosa. When our daughter went down to a critical level at just 12 years of age, existing on 5 cornflakes and a sherry glass of water a day, we found out the hard way that her medical needs had never been addressed, despite being within the mental health service.

As parents, we were devastated to think that our daughter might not have survived and the words of the consultant paediatrician haunt me to this day.

"If you don't eat you will die, if you don't drink you will die quicker."

Fortunately, our daughter survived that time but deteriorated to a critical level 3 more times after that.

As parents, we educated ourselves, identified the gaps in services, and became proactive in the development of Eating Disorder Services in Hull and East Riding.

On 1st September 2000, we opened our doors to support others and, in 2004, we founded Seed Eating Disorder Support Services (Support and Empathy for people with Eating Disorders) charity, supporting sufferers and carers of this devastating illness. And work tirelessly to make a difference to others and provide a service like no other. A service that saves lives.

In June 2010, I was honoured to receive an MBE from the Queen for services to eating disorders, perhaps one of the proudest moments in my life, up there with giving birth to my four children and seeing our seven grandchildren born.

On 27th January 2023, we will officially open our new Resource Room within the Princes Quay in Hull for the benefit of local people and those countrywide.

I was honoured when Emma, author of 'Slaying Monsters, Dodging Doughnuts' approached me to write the foreword. This book is an essential read for anyone affected by anorexia nervosa: carers, parents, family and friends.

It is a mother's heartbreaking account of the highs and lows of supporting a loved one through an eating disorder. From the opening paragraph, I was transported back to our journey my heart aching for others struggling and their loved ones caring.

As in our experience, Emma shares her painful, yet inspirational, story of how her daughter nearly died from the illness. She sheds light on the profound effect on anyone who is part of the sufferer's life, including parents, grandparents, siblings, friends, and loved ones.

Eating disorders have the highest mortality rate of any mental health illness, with a staggering 20% of people dying as a direct result of their illness, or through suicide.

It is a complex illness to treat and, sadly, the healthcare profession, unless specialised, knows very little about the needs of the sufferer or those that support them. Excuse the pun but one size does not fit all. It is not uncommon for supporters to feel alone. Emma has written her story and shared her challenges so that others can take comfort that they are not alone in this fight.

This book has it all, from the devastating impact that an eating disorder can bring, to the tears, the laughter, the giggles, the doughnuts (I won't spoil that for you), and the great tips that Emma used to keep motivated and hopeful to help her daughter.

My greatest passion is to educate people about the dangers of medical risks of eating disorders, and I am proud of the service Seed offers to make a difference to others. Slaying Monsters, Dodging Doughnuts is a much-needed, encouraging and supportive read from a mother's perspective.

I wish Emma and her family all the very best for the future. I wish you the same, whatever your struggles.

Marg Oaten MBE

January 2023

My Dear Friend,

Since you are reading this, I assume that either you or someone you care about is dealing with this cruel illness. Or maybe you want to learn about an eating disorder and its impact on a person, and their family.

I will share our journey and what helped me when I was struggling. I hope that you might find something to help you.

I can't be there in person, but I hope you will see that I am with you along the way as that friend you can turn to. If you are affected by this illness, either directly or indirectly, I am incredibly sorry. I am sending all my love and support to help you through it.

This is my honest account of navigating through this journey with my daughter, Poppy, and her anorexia. Each one of us will have different experiences and struggles. I am not a trained eating disorder professional. I am an ordinary mum who wants to share her story to help you feel less alone and hopeless. You may find something that will restore and maintain your hope, strength, and motivation to keep on fighting to free your loved one.

Many times, I have had to pause amidst the relentless battles and have lost my focus on trying to free Poppy from the illness. I have wanted to give up. Despite being heavily bruised, battered and frightened, I have always risen again and found the strength to continue to support her, so that she can choose how she wants to live and not be dictated by her thoughts and beliefs that heavily impose themselves on her.

You too may experience or witness moments of despair, uncertain of what can be done to help free your loved one from this devastating illness. I have had many of those moments.

You, or your loved one, might want to give up and run away, even if it's for a short time to escape from it all. That was me.

Some days, you might hate your life and grieve for the life you have lost. That was also me.

You may experience guilt, blame or shame. I have experienced all of these. I will share more about this as we go through my story.

Maybe you are struggling to see ahead. You might not believe it but, wherever you are on your journey, better days can happen.

The journey my daughter and I found ourselves on at times has sucked every last bit of energy from us. It was all-consuming and has sapped our strength, hope, and resilience, but it never took away our love for each other.

Keep holding on, my friend. I am here with you, willing you to keep going. Willing for you to keep holding on and believing that you can get through this. We can do this together.

As I said before, I am just a plain Jane, an ordinary mum to my daughter and her older brother, Jordan. There is nothing special about me, other than the love I have for my children. I don't have all the answers. Most of the time, I feel I don't have any.

We are not completely free yet, but I still have hope. Hope that soon we will be.

I've been pummelled down by the exhaustion of each day, each challenge, and each agonising battle. I know that there will be more of those days, but I refuse to give in. I refuse to fall and not get back up until we eventually win.

Poppy will get her life back and so will I. If I can do this, then so can you. Come with me on my journey and let's do it together.

Let me start by sharing my story, where it all began.

Introduction

"Her heart could give up at any minute."

That was the most terrifying news they gave me.

I only had Poppy in my life for fourteen years. That was not long enough. Selfishly, I wanted more.

Waves of emotion flooded me and brought me to my knees. My heart was pounding, my hands were clammy, and my tummy was churning. I started to sob quietly before uncontrollable tears pooled out of my eyes.

My mind raced for my poor Poppy.

Why?

How did this happen?

Why didn't I notice?

What am I going to do?

What are they going to do?

What do I tell her brother?

What do I say to her?

I didn't see that coming, and then it was too late. I was petrified that she was going to die. No one expects a child to die before them.

My head pounded with fear. Fear of losing the future with my daughter, fear of missing out on watching and nurturing her as she grew, and fear of missing seeing her develop into a young woman.

I wouldn't witness her accomplishments. I wouldn't see her achieving her hopes and dreams. I wouldn't be able to celebrate any more birthdays with her. I would miss meeting her first love, her graduation and her wedding day.

I was scared of the life in front of me, without her.

How can I live without her?

How can we live without her?

How had we got here?

Where had it gone wrong?

Was it too late for her?

Could she pull through?

1

Hold on Poppy

Poppy was lying in the hospital. She was alone. It still hadn't sunk in but seeing her body so frail brought it all back to me. It was real. She could die at any minute.

They told us that her heart was incompatible with life. What! Fear didn't come close to describing the emotions I felt.

I couldn't get my head around it, as she had only been on the ward a week and it was only two weeks since she had first seen the eating disorder team. Within a short space of time, she had deteriorated so quickly to the point where her life was on the line.

"Her heart could give up at any minute," they said. That phrase kept going around and around in my head.

I could lose my daughter.

Never in my wildest nightmares did I think that would happen to us. I always assumed that I would die first. Even though, as a parent, you know there are no guarantees in life, it still doesn't prepare you for the fact that your child could die. I knew life was fragile, but I never really gave it much thought.

Nearly every single moment of my day was taken up thinking about her, willing her to keep living, hoping that she would make it out alive. I didn't want to be another statistic. I didn't want to be another parent who had lost their child to anorexia.

Each morning, I opened my eyes with trepidation. Had she made it through the night? What will today bring?

I dreaded the phone ringing, hoping that it wasn't the hospital with bad news.

My mind was constantly bombarded by an avalanche of thoughts of memories, conversations, what-ifs and shoulds. I couldn't silence the constant babble in my head.

I should have spotted the signs.

I should have been able to turn this around quickly.

I should have been a better mum.

I should have been more present in her life.

I should have eaten with her more.

My days were flooded with feelings of guilt, disbelief, and anger at myself for missing the illness, as well as inconsolable fear of losing my daughter, my baby. My eyes were constantly sore due to all the tears I shed, worrying that she wouldn't make it through another night.

I couldn't stop the questions forever repeating in my mind:

When did it start?

Why did it start?

How did I miss it?

What did I do wrong?

Why didn't I see it?

Was I too focused on myself?

Family members would unhelpfully add to my feelings of inadequacy, and I used that as a stick to beat myself further.

I felt helpless and useless. There was nothing I could do. We were in the hands of the hospital and it was going to take time. Time for her body to hopefully get stronger and time for her brain to repair.

Out of fear, out of desperation, and out of other options, I prayed.

I prayed that she would live.

Hold on, Poppy.

Please hold on.

2

Knocked sideways

S aying it out loud didn't make it any easier.

"Poppy has anorexia."

I never imagined that we would be in that situation. It wasn't something that was on my radar. No one I knew had an eating disorder, and I wasn't aware of any of Poppy's friends having eating issues. It wasn't a topic that had ever come up in the house. The only time I was aware of anorexia was when, as a child, I watched the story of Karen Carpenter. Then, as a teenager, I remembered reflecting on her talent and thinking how awful it was that her life had ended so tragically short.

I didn't expect it at all. I didn't look for it, as I didn't think I needed to. I just didn't think about it at all.

I wish I had. I wish I had seen the signs more clearly and quickly. If I had, maybe we wouldn't have been in this situation.

How did it go so wrong, so quickly?

Fourteen years had flown by, and it seemed so long ago since she was a baby. Nothing prepares you for the love you feel when they are placed into your arms for the first time. That precious little bundle was ours to look after, to protect, to show her what was right and wrong, to guide her and always be there for her.

How I wish I could go back to those younger years and start all over again, and somehow do it differently so that I would have done a better job of looking out for her. If only I could change things. But I couldn't. Nothing was going to change where she was at.

I replayed event after event in my mind, looking for clues that I had missed. Each year, she would stop eating chocolate and biscuits for Lent, but that was nothing new. What was new was the fact that her Easter eggs remained untouched, which was unusual as Poppy loved eating sweets and biscuits. She had a sweet tooth, just like me. Poppy and I enjoyed puddings when we went out for food; that was the norm for us.

When the Covid pandemic struck, Poppy found it hard being at home all the time. It didn't help that I was working full-time from home. Work was hectic, and my online meetings usually started at 8 am and often finished around 6 pm, with little breaks for lunch and little time to grab a drink. Eating together was impossible but, unknown to me, this gave Poppy the perfect opportunity to restrict herself.

I didn't see it until it was too late. I saw her anxiety increase, which seemed to relate to the amount of homework. She was fixated on the fact that each piece of homework had to be perfect and nothing less would do. She was overwhelmed with the deadlines and being at home rather than at school. She was taking longer to complete the homework, which ultimately added more pressure. No amount of teachers' support enabled her to budge from her perfectionism, and the pressure she put on herself.

As life continued to be busy for both of us, mealtimes gradually got later and, before we knew it, it would be 7 - 8 pm before we had our tea. On the odd occasion it was after this and Poppy would tell me it was too late to have a big meal, as she was going to bed. I didn't think much about it, I just put it down to us being busy, and made a mental note to get back into a better routine.

It was a refreshing change to see Poppy spend time with her friends, as she seemed brighter and more like herself. Everything seemed better. I hadn't realised it, at the time, but I had made it worse. I was encouraging her to spend time with her friends and, unknown to me, she was eating very little and what she ate had not fuelled the amount of energy she needed to walk to her friends and back. She admitted much later that she didn't know how she had walked that distance, as she would often feel weak, exhausted, and faint. How did I not see that? It was too scary to consider that her heart could have given up whilst she was walking.

I had no reason to consider anything was wrong with her eating, as sitting down for a family meal at the weekend was still part of our routine, and she was still eating puddings with me. Eating meat began to be more of an issue but I could relate to that, as I was not much older than her when I stopped eating red meat. I didn't give that much thought.

She would tell me that she had eaten. She left her dirty bowls and cutlery out on the side, and crumbs were still on the table, so there was nothing new there. I still didn't consider anything to be wrong.

Little did I know that she has been taking every opportunity to skip or restrict meals whenever she could. I always felt lucky that Poppy and I had an honest relationship and I had no reason to think otherwise.

One day I noticed that she was upset because she had eaten too many biscuits. There were also a few occasions when I picked her up from school early and she hadn't eaten all her lunch, and there were times when she began to talk about trying to be good and not eat many sweet things. I didn't think much about it at the time. I stressed the importance of eating her lunch and told her that no food was good or bad.

During Covid, everyone seemed to be talking about, and joining in with the online fitness classes that had started. It was a nice thing for us to do together. Poppy was more dedicated than me and would exercise two or three times a week, which seemed reasonable. I did question her when that increased to four or five times a week. I spent time explaining the importance of resting your body, and the need to not exercise too much. I began to feel uneasy when I noticed she was exercising every day, and I asked her not to do any more as she needed to rest. She agreed.

By then, my instinct was too loud to ignore. Something was not right. No one should exercise every day.

Disagreements started with what she wanted to eat, as she no longer fancied any of her favourite foods, preferring salads. More noticeable was her increasing anxiety around mealtimes.

I couldn't put my finger on it. Her moods were getting worse, and I found myself having to walk on eggshells. When it came to preparing meals, she wouldn't leave the kitchen, and she would question every ingredient, and reason with me about the portion sizes, telling me that she was not hungry, or was feeling poorly. That was so unlike her.

Something didn't add up.

Too many times she had eaten on her own rather than wait for me.

Too many times she had left some food saying she was full.

Too many times she had pushed her food around the plate and got grumpier if I asked her to eat more.

I began to be more vigilant, more to reassure myself that everything was OK, rather than to confirm it.

I couldn't shake the nagging doubt that she was staging things to throw me off. The knife looked as if it had been dipped in butter, the cereal bowl was too clean for her to have eaten her breakfast, and the crumbs looked as if they had been strategically placed on the plate.

Mealtimes were getting more upsetting for her and she kept refusing to eat all her food, saying that she was too full or felt unwell. For a while, I rarely saw her eating crisps or puddings.

Did she have an eating disorder?

I didn't want to believe it but she was more stressed with eating, her portion sizes were getting smaller and she continued to make excuses. Something was wrong, and I couldn't think what else it could be. It had to be an eating disorder.

I then noticed she had a pear-drop odour. I used to smell it when she was poorly as a young girl, so I put it down to the fact that she must be coming down with something and thought nothing more of it.

My head was in a spin worrying about her, so I rang the doctor's surgery and was given a telephone appointment that day. I expressed my concerns. Poppy's anxiety was worsening, and I was worried about her eating and level of distress. I asked if it could be an eating disorder.

The doctor didn't confirm or deny that she had. She dismissed my query about being referred to Child and Adolescent Mental Health Services (CAMHS) by saying that there was a long waiting list, and it would be months before she could be seen. Instead, she advised me to look at several websites and contact a local number that might help. I was advised to take Poppy to the clinic in three months.

I was bewildered, as she didn't even offer to check her at the clinic. She didn't seem concerned about her at all.

Was I being overprotective? Maybe there was nothing wrong, but my feelings told me differently.

The referral form was sent off that day, as the quicker we got help the better. They were quick to respond but said that they couldn't see Poppy as her BMI was too low. I suggested that, before they rejected the referral, I would check her weight and height at the surgery as my scales were not accurate. The nurse worked out her BMI and confirmed that it was too low for them to see her. Her urine had ketones present, which explained the pear-drop smell. She explained that Poppy's body was eating its fat reserves for energy due to the lack of nutrition, confirming that she had been restricting food for some time. She had complained of feeling cold during the previous few days, which was unlike Poppy. I did not know it at the time but that was her body's way of protecting her main organs.

That knocked me sideways.

I was in denial, hoping that I was wrong, but the facts were clear to see. The low weight, the distress at mealtimes, the excessive exercise, the mood changes, the coldness and the ketones in her urine. It takes time for a body to use up its reserves, so it was clear that she had been restricting her food intake for some time.

I hadn't realised, although I had an inkling. I had looked at the events in isolation but unfortunately had failed to join the dots. It wasn't helpful that she hid her body under baggy clothes, making any weight loss difficult to spot until it was too late. It can be a manipulative and deceitful illness, which makes it very difficult to see the whole picture.

When we were given the diagnosis of anorexia, I read anything and everything I could. I joined groups and attended workshops. I immersed myself in finding anything that could help. There was not one day where I didn't read something, or attend something, and my days were consumed with information about eating disorders.

Within a week, the CAMHS eating disorder team contacted us to gain some insight into where Poppy was at. I held back my tears as I heard Poppy share some of the details. They were going to discuss her case at their weekly meeting and would get back to us. Meanwhile, they advised her to stop walking and to rest as much as possible. Her eyes filled with tears when she heard that. I didn't know, at that time, how deep she was in the illness then.

It went from bad to worse. I knew we were in trouble when I saw her sobbing inconsolably, and no amount of encouragement or hugs could get her to eat one satsuma segment. Normally she would have devoured a bowl of fruit in minutes and asked for more, whereas then it was as if I was trying to get her to eat something poisonous.

I tried everything I could think of, and explained that our bodies need a certain amount of energy. I spoke about the analogy of a car needing the right fuel, otherwise it would stop in its tracks. I pleaded with her. I tried distracting her with videos, clips, and anything I could think of.

Nothing worked.

The amount she was eating became smaller, and she moaned and groaned when I refused to allow her to walk. Her body was getting thinner, her face was gaunter and paler, and her legs looked as if they could snap at any minute.

No longer was there any joy or fun in Poppy. The happiness had been drained out of her and was replaced with sadness, anxiety, anger, frustration, denial and guilt. Her life was consumed by calorie counting, excessive exercise, excessive standing, bodychecking, and self-loathing. She had an insatiable focus on losing more weight and checking to see her ribs.

That wasn't the Poppy we knew.

I was scared.

3

Monsters do exist

As a child, the very thought of monsters terrified me, so I would throw my duvet over my head in a rush whenever I felt them lurking. Growing up, I soon realised that monsters didn't exist. Little did I know that, at an older age, I would believe in them again.

It felt like we were in our own horror movie. You know the movie I mean where the main character is in trouble and oblivious to the baddie who is out to get them. You start shouting at the screen, willing them to run and not look back.

The difference is that the 'baddie' is an eating disorder (ED), which wasn't the type of monster that I thought of as a 6-year-old child. I was oblivious that this invisible monster was taking my daughter as its next victim. It was slowly circling her, slowly drawing her in and taking control of her mind. I wasn't even screaming for her to run away from it, as I didn't see it come for her until it was too late.

Monsters do exist! There was one in my daughter's head.

But I couldn't hide under the duvet. I couldn't ask my dad to run upstairs and check everything was clear before I went to sleep. I was the only one who could rid us of that monster.

It had wrapped itself around my loved one, drawing her closer in its grasp, posing as her friend, making her feel whole and complete again. Every minute, day, week, month and year, it carefully manipulated her so that she had less and less control over her thoughts until I no longer recognised her.

It started off being her friend, being there for her when she thought she had no one else. Initially, it said the nicest things, befriending her and making her feel better about herself. It offered comfort, safety, and a promise of a better life, before gradually revealing its true blackened colours. By then it was too late, she was too invested, too consumed and too controlled. It switched from being a supportive friend to a baddie in the blink of an eye, and the promise it offered lingered.

Stepping away from the ED felt impossible, scary and unnecessary. Staying with it felt like the only option. The belittling attacks and bullying continued to trick her into thinking she was no longer good enough, that she was fat, no one liked her, she was a burden to everyone and would be better off dead.

It started to take more control and put the following questions in her mind:

> "Why don't you leave some of your lunch? You will feel better."
>
> "Why don't you stop eating chocolate and biscuits? They are fattening."
>
> "Why don't you miss a meal or two? It can't hurt."

It was very convincing and manipulative, saying anything to keep her under its control and nothing anyone else said was able to make a difference.

How can a fight be won against a monster you can't see? It had constant access to her, 24 hours a day and 7 days a week. She was engulfed by its world, and no amount of persuasion, cajoling, or nagging could break the ED's hold.

Lying in the hospital bed, it was clear to see that she was becoming its next victim.

4

Help was on its way

I longed for Monday so that I could call the eating disorder team and ask for urgent help. I sobbed and sobbed, whilst trying to explain how much she had deteriorated.

They arranged to see Poppy later that day, when they would check her thoroughly and put her on a meal plan. The relief was enormous, knowing that they were there to help. It was going to be OK, and things were going to turn around.

But the ED had different ideas. It was so strong and loud, and Poppy became argumentative. I couldn't get her out of the kitchen, she was my shadow watching me all the time, what I did, what I was using in the cooking and how much food I plated up for her. She was given a 30-minute time limit to eat. The distress of eating was unrelenting for her, it was present at every mealtime.

I panicked seeing her come downstairs. Her face was much paler than normal, and her lips were blue. She looked as if she was going to faint and I rang the GP. Her blood pressure and heart rate were low but on the normal side of low. Phew, panic over.

Monday came and Poppy was so quiet in the car. I suspected that she was anxiously pondering what CAMHS would do. The mood lightened when we saw photos of the very cute and cuddly puppy that my friend had just brought home. Without thinking, I sent her a text back asking if they had any left. There was one black and white female, and she was so cute. I asked Poppy what she thought we should do. Should we get her?

That was the first time I had given any thought to getting a dog. I knew I was grasping at straws, as I was desperate to find something to give her focus, and to give her something to smile and laugh about. To give all of us something other than what we had at that point.

I was also worried about what was in front of us. Thankfully, I was able to see reason and I listened to Poppy. She made sense, as she wanted to wait until she was better before getting a puppy. So we put our name down for another litter that was due some months later, which gave Poppy an incentive.

At the CAMHS appointment, I could sense something wasn't right from the looks they gave each other. They wanted to admit her as her heart rate and blood pressure were a concern. I was in shock. A week ago her stats were fine. I wasn't sure how she could deteriorate so quickly in such a short space of time. I wasn't expecting that.

There wasn't much time to think as we were led into Reception whilst they prepared a hospital bed. Poppy sobbed and sobbed. She pleaded to go home, she pleaded to be given one last chance, and she pleaded for me to talk to them. I was torn from feeling some relief that they were doing something, yet upset by Poppy's pleas to go home.

We just held each other. Leaving her on the ward was difficult, as she looked so anxious. She was attached to a heart monitor and on bed rest. Much to her disgust, she was no longer able to walk to the bathroom. It was sad to see three more girls on the ward suffering from the same illness, all at different stages of recovery. One had not long been admitted, another had been there nine weeks and the other had been there nearly twelve weeks. I had assumed it would only be a few weeks until Poppy would be home, but that made me unsure.

5

What was it like for Poppy?

My perception of what Poppy was going through wasn't even close. It took me some time to truly understand what it was like for her. We never really know what someone else is going through, as each person's experience is different.

Imagine that you are being bombarded with thoughts from when you get up in the morning until the moment you go to bed. Not positive uplifting thoughts, but thoughts filled with hatred and self-loathing such as, "That's not good enough", "You are stupid", "You are selfish", "You are useless", "You would be better dead than alive", "You are a burden", "No one loves you", "You are a pig eating that food". "You are going to be so fat", "No one will want you, no one will love you". And there is no rest from it. Now add into the mix others asking you to sit down at the table, where you'll face the fear that scares you the most. Not just once, but up to 3-6 times a day.

The noise inside your head increases and the chatter from those around you grows louder and more frequent, all multiplying in intensity. Your body flips into a flight or fight response. Your breathing feels heavy, palpitations begin, heat rises throughout your body, your hands get clammy and your tummy churns to the point of agony. You start to feel sick and the pain spreads. Everything becomes a blur. They are telling you to sit down and eat. Pain intensifies and reaches a crescendo. All you want to do is run. Run from the pain. Run from everyone. You want it to stop. You can't concentrate on what people are saying. You can't think clearly.

The only way you can stop the pain is to restrict what you eat. Your mind tells you to crumble the food and hide it. "They won't notice." You start to crumble the food and you notice that the voice inside your head is praising you.

You know the only way for the pain to stop is to obey the voice. You know from experience that if you don't obey the voice, the comments will become louder, more belittling and more destructive. Each comment rips more away from you. You give up hope that you will ever be free of the voice. You feel that you have no choice but to give in, as you just want a moment of peace.

How would you feel? Would you want to eat that food? Would you feel great or drained and exhausted? Would you want to do it all again after a few hours?

Unfortunately, that is what Poppy and many others experience every day, with every snack and every meal.

My heart goes out to everyone going through this. The only way they can be free from this illness is to go through the pain and confront what they are scared about. I have so much respect for them. They are courageous people, who have to get up each day and face their fear time and time again. That is exactly what Poppy must do to be free.

6

We are worried about you Poppy

The house was so quiet without Poppy. My time had been consumed with supporting her. I was lost and didn't know what to do with myself.

I was so tired from our battles. I found resting was not something I could do freely. I couldn't put my mind to anything and even the simplest of tasks seemed difficult. Thoughts constantly churned in my mind, and I was barely surviving on a few hours of sleep most nights.

However, for the first time in ages, I felt relief in having no responsibility for her eating. I was just Mum. The Play Staff on the ward were amazing, sitting with Poppy, encouraging her to eat, and engaging her in activities to help distract her from the pain she experienced afterwards.

I was confused to see her having a glass of water for a snack. Surely it needed to be food? The staff explained that they needed to slowly increase her food intake to reduce the chances of Refeeding Syndrome, which could be fatal. Each day, I glanced at the record of what she had eaten, and each day I read, 'refused, eaten only a few mouthfuls'.

It was our first MDT (Multi-disciplinary team) meeting since being on the ward and Poppy felt overwhelmed seeing so many people there. They discussed her stats. Her heart rate and blood pressure had worsened, and she had lost more weight.

"We are worried about you, Poppy," they said. "We are worried that your heart could give up at any minute."

They explained that Poppy's heart rate went as low as 27 beats per minute. It should be around 50-60 beats per minute. I was scared, really scared.

I couldn't hold it back anymore and I cried. I could lose her. I was stunned. I had expected her to be getting better. I expected to take her home soon. 27 beats per minute! I hadn't expected that.

They explained that they wanted Poppy to gain a certain amount of weight each week, and they were going to introduce a Fortisip drink to the meal plan to help stabilise her heart rate. To Poppy, that was her worst nightmare come true. She was being forced to eat and gain weight.Hearing that, she zoned out and retracted into her inner world.

I was relieved that they were doing something.

When it was just the two of us on the ward, she cried and cried. Her fears were clear to see. I couldn't do anything other than hold her. I put on a brave face and told her that it would be OK, that we would get through it. I meant it but I didn't know how.

I held onto the hope that they would fix her.

I held onto the hope that they would be able to turn it around quickly.

I held onto the hope that we would give us our lives back.

I couldn't stop blaming myself. She was only fourteen and was too young to die. She was too young to know the implications of what she was doing.

I should have noticed.

I should have done more.

I should have prevented it from happening.

I didn't know much about anorexia.

I didn't know that it had the highest mortality rate for mental health disorders.

I didn't know if she would make it through.

Not knowing if she would make it through another day took its toll on me. My mind continued with the constant chatter that couldn't be silenced at night. I couldn't get it out of my mind that I might lose her. Could today be the day that she died? I looked drained, l lacked lustre for life and continued to struggle to concentrate. It became more noticeable to others as time went on.

I reached out to John, a good friend who has been a father figure since I lost my dad at 27. He said he would pray for Poppy. I had lost some faith when my dad died, as it had hit me hard. It's interesting how, when you are desperate, you go back to what you know, and will do anything, in the hope that it will help. John and his Christian friends continued to keep us in their thoughts and prayers, giving me the comfort that I needed.

It helped my sanity to see Poppy every day. I missed her being at home. Some days we just sat and watched the staff busying around, some days we cuddled and chatted, and some days we played games. Often, she was too tired to do anything.

It was soon Monday again.

Poppy dreaded Mondays. Her anxiety would start to build towards the end of the week until it was at an all-time high for the MDT meeting.

Another week had gone. She had gained some weight and they called it 'on plan'. That was good news. No change to her stats but at least we were heading in the right direction. Poppy hated hearing that as, to her, it brought pain in a way I couldn't imagine.

Unknown to me at the time, the ED's thoughts had intensified to a whole new level. It was downright evil to her. It would say anything at all to belittle her, telling her repeatedly that they would make her fat, that she was lazy, and that she was ugly. There was no let-up. She was completely sucked in, and despite just being told she could die, she believed her ED thoughts 100%. She couldn't see how ill she was, or how weak her body had become.

At the next MDT, she had lost weight and her meal plan was increased as a result. I was baffled at how she had done this as she was still bed-bound and attached to a heart monitor, and her activity was pretty much zero. They asked her if she knew why she had lost weight. I looked at them, perplexed. How could she have done anything? She told them that she didn't know.

Consoling Poppy was an impossible task after the MDT, as her emotions were a mixture of anger, despair and fear. She dreaded seeing the dietician as she knew that her meal plan would be increased again.

Another week passed and Poppy lost more weight. I still didn't understand how it was possible.

7

No one prepared me

No one prepared me for the journey ahead.

No one said that there would be days when I would feel alone, desperate, guilty, angry, frustrated, lost, broken and defeated.

No one prepared me for anything like that.

I wish that someone had taken me to one side in the early days and told me that it was going to be my worst nightmare, that my life would be consumed by the illness, day and night. That I would need to fight, and keep fighting, for my loved one. She would not be able to fight for herself because the illness had taken hold of her, like a hostage.

I wish they had said that there would be days when I would have nothing in me to fight but that was OK. On those days, I could just pause and be kind to myself.

I wish they had explained the importance of self-care and the need to recharge.

It would have helped if I had been told, so I have listed a few tips for you.

★ If you have any inkling that someone might have an eating disorder, seek help as soon as you can. If no one is listening, keep asking for help until someone does.

★ Keep a sense of humour, as you are going to need it.

★ Don't be afraid to get help for yourself. It is not a sign of weakness. It shows that you are strong.

★ Lean on family and friends.

★ Find a support group that you can share openly with.

★ Recovery is not a straight line. It is frustrating watching your loved one go up and down, taking one or two steps forwards followed by many steps backwards.

★ This isn't going to be easy, but you can get through it and better days will happen. Embrace those better days and relish the good moments, as they can help you get through the more difficult times.

8

Why doesn't anyone listen to me?

20th July 2020

Dear Diary,

Why doesn't anyone listen to me?

Another dreadful meeting in the hospital. We sat there, waiting for them to say if there had been any changes or any hope to cling to. My daughter's life is in the balance of these strangers.

She lost weight. How can she lose weight? She is bed-bound, and she is eating, not a lot but more than she did. She was asked if there was any reason why she had lost weight. She muttered, "No." I wanted to believe her.

"No improvements to her heart", they said.

So many questions were buzzing around in my head but time felt pressured as they had another one to see. No time to ask questions. No one asked if I had any questions. They had already decided what they were going to do.

The meal plan was increased. The inevitable meltdown started.

"But what about her heart?" I wanted to scream. But it was too late. We were back on the ward.

No one seemed to be free to answer my questions. Nurses and doctors were busy seeing patients. They didn't seem to notice our pain. It felt as if no one cared.

Poppy was so angry. I haven't seen her that angry in a long while. I was unable to console her. With more weight loss, her meal plan had been increased. She had to stay in bed and use the wheelchair to go to the bathroom.

How could I leave her when she is crying? I had to go back to work, but she needed me. My heart was torn. Torn between wanting to hug her and wanting to plead with her to stop exercising. She admitted it. She had been doing a few jumps in the bathroom. I felt as if I had been kicked in the stomach.

> Her body was so weak that even a few jumps were enough to lose weight.
> Why couldn't she see that?
> Why couldn't she see how frail her body was?
> Why couldn't she see that she could die?

There are no signs of her getting better. I can't believe that she was exercising. I wanted to scream at her, I desperately wanted her to realise what she was doing. How could I get her to see how serious it was?

It is so frustrating. It is a long waiting game. Another week will have to go by, hoping that she won't exercise, hoping that she will eat all her food, and hoping that she will gain weight. That we will see some improvement, any improvement. Week after week, no weight gain. Four weeks and no further forward.

When are things going to get better?

Her friends are not aware of where she is. Her friends are able to live their lives, have fun, and be teenagers. Whereas, she is stuck in the hospital, bed-bound.

There is no fun, no joy, just torment. Her life had been robbed by this illness.

They are not aware that she is so poorly and fighting for her life. Well, that's not true. I am fighting for her, against the ED which is forcing her to exercise and not eat. Is she fighting with me or against me? I am not sure.

But it is a battle that we must win.

9

Why can't she see?

It was hard visiting her every day, looking and hoping for any signs that she was there somewhere and that she was fighting against the ED. I glanced at her notes in anticipation, checking her blood pressure and heart rate observations. That familiar feeling of disappointment hit me when I saw that only half of the meal had been eaten and her pudding had been refused again.

When was she going to eat?

When were things going to improve?

I pleaded with her continually to fight. To eat and not let the ED win. I asked her to do it for me, for her brother and her nanna. I knew I was wasting my time, but I had to try. I had to try and find something that would reach her.

She looked so weak and pale, her fingers were so thin, and her face so gaunt. I could feel her spine when I cuddled her, and it sent a shiver down me. How did she get so skinny? Why did she even want to be? She was a shadow of who she used to be. There was no recognition within her that she was ill, and she thought everyone was overreacting.

Why couldn't she see what I did?

Why couldn't she see what it was doing to her?

I wish she could. I needed her to see what I could see. I needed her to stop exercising, and start eating. I didn't know how long I could keep going, seeing her becoming thinner and weaker.

I kept asking myself how could the fight be won against an invisible monster? It had constant access to her. I only saw her for three hours a day in the hospital. I felt powerless. I knew it was not for me to keep fighting. But it was hard not to.

I pleaded with the staff to help but they told me that therapy wouldn't work if her brain was starved. The only way for her to get better was to eat. It was a waiting game.

Did anyone see how hard it was for me?

I dreaded those Monday meetings. I knew I should start the day positively but it was hard when, for the last few weeks, she had made little or no progress. I came away with so many unanswered questions. It felt so rushed and they only wanted to hear from her, not from me.

Why didn't they listen to me?

Please hold on my darling, I need you.

10

Believe in the power of hope

Hope.
It was all I had.

I had to hold on to something.

I hoped that they were wrong.
I hoped that she would start eating again properly.
I hoped that they could make her better quickly.

Hope was all I had.

I hoped that she would be free again.
I hoped that we would get our lives back.
I hoped that one day this would be a distant memory.

I didn't want to think that she couldn't get through this.
I didn't want to think that she couldn't beat this illness.
I didn't want to think that she could die.

I needed her to live.
I needed to have hope that she would.
I needed to believe in the power of hope.

Sometimes a flicker of hope was all I had to get me through.

Some days it felt as if the flicker had been extinguished and I was left with hopelessness. I was stuck thinking about how bad the situation was and that she was unlikely to get better.

I found myself staying in a state of hopelessness, for fear of being disappointed. It was easier to stay there than to expect something good to happen.

Reaching out to others in a similar situation made me look at things from a different perspective. I couldn't change that Poppy's life was hanging in the balance, but I could change how I felt about it, so I started to be open to her survival.

11

Mum, I want to die, sorry!

Seeing your loved one in so much distress is unbearable.

Poppy's brain had been starved and needed to be repaired. Food was the medicine. Yet the one thing that would help her was the one thing that was hurting her. It upset me to my core to see my loved one in such pain. I couldn't take it away. I wanted to fix it so badly but I couldn't. I watched helplessly.

Every bit of oxygen was sucked out of my body when my daughter told me that she wanted to die. Life to her was no longer worth living. The pain was excruciating and the only way to end it was to end her life. That was my baby.

When she hurt herself as a toddler, a magic cuddle or a magic plaster made everything OK. Not this time. There was no magic fix. I wished I could take all the pain away. I would have done it in the blink of an eye. I wished I could swap bodies to give her a rest.

Poppy chose to hide her pain from the staff. She felt that she wasn't ill enough to be there. She felt she didn't deserve any help and was a burden to everyone. Her self-esteem and self-worth had been eroded. I found it incredibly difficult to see her like that and to read her texts. As hard as I tried, I couldn't shrug off the impact of those dark messages.

I hated seeing her at such a low point in her life.

I was beyond tired of trying to be cheery and positive. As much as I was holding on, I felt my resilience begin to crack. Slowly at first but, with each message I received, it cracked a bit more. Each one reminded me of how much pain she was in.

"Keep it short, and change the subject," they advised me in my responses to Poppy. That was not always easy to do, especially when the message read, "Mum, I want to die, sorry!"

In moments like that, I felt alone. It felt as if I had been kicked in the tummy. I read it again in the hope that I had misunderstood it. I hadn't.

I sobbed and sobbed. I had nearly lost her and then she wanted to give up and die. I panicked. I tried ringing her, but there was no answer. I messaged her to ring me back. I didn't know what to do. I waited and waited for what seemed like forever, but it had only been a few minutes. I tried ringing her again, but no answer. I rang the ward to make sure she was OK. They said she wasn't in her bed.

My panic was at a new level. Where was she? No one knew. I was scared that she had done something. I could hear them asking other staff members where she was. No one had seen her. My tummy was in knots, my mouth was dry, and my legs wouldn't stop shaking. Where was she?

After what seemed like an hour, they had found her. One of the staff had taken her to a side room. The relief was amazing, but it took me some time to calm down. I was so glad to hear that she was safe. I couldn't wait to see her that afternoon.

I couldn't understand why she wasn't having any therapy, as she needed help. Even Poppy recognised that she needed help. They explained that her brain was too starved, and her cognition too impaired for therapy to help. The only thing that would make a difference was ensuring she had the right nutrition. They often repeated that food was medicine, which was something she came to hate people saying, but it was true. It is what she needed at that time.

I don't think anyone appreciated how hard it was for me to just sit and watch my child suffer in front of my eyes and I couldn't help in any way, other than wait for the medicine to work.

It was a slow waiting game.

12

What would I have changed?

Fourteen years had flown by. It seemed such a long time since she was a baby.

How I wished so many times that I could start all over again. But if I could have gone back in time, what would I have changed?

I didn't know. I had never spoken about dieting, and no foods had been forbidden. I had tried not to label food as good or bad. Cakes, biscuits and chocolate were as readily available as fruit and vegetables in our house. Poppy equally loved eating fruit and sweets.

However, I hadn't realised that, indirectly, I had been labelling food. It took Poppy to tell me that, when asked if I wanted a biscuit or a pudding, my answer sometimes would have been, "No, thank you, I am trying to be good." I hadn't thought about it until Poppy pointed it out. I hadn't thought about the impact that it would have.

I now notice conversations that people have about diets, wanting to lose weight, how much weight they have gained and how to stop gaining weight. I hadn't noticed before but I now cringe as this was a big trigger for Poppy and reinforced her fear of food and gaining weight.

I hadn't realised the impact of social media and it is something I would change. I gave in when Poppy begged me to have a social media account like her friends. I wish now that I hadn't. Despite talking about the dangers and that what we see isn't always reality, it didn't provide enough protection. I didn't realise that, unknowingly, she was being exposed to the pressure of society to look a certain way.

How do we protect our loved ones from this pressure?

I am not sure. Social media has a big influence on teenagers and Poppy was slowly drawn into that world. Unknown to me, she was beginning to feel unhappy about her appearance. It is too easy to spend a lot of time on our phones. I often scroll through my phone, losing time.

I had let the busyness of life get in the way, and we often ate separately.

It is not always possible to find a cause for an eating disorder. These things may have contributed to it, but there was a lot more to it. Going back in time was not the answer, even though I desperately wanted to start all over again.

Maybe the experience needed to happen, although it is hard to understand why. So far, a lot of good has come out of it. We have met many lovely people. We are making some changes, sitting down together more, trying to have less tech time, and keeping the dialogue open especially about triggers to help support Poppy.

13

Monday blues

Oh no, it was Monday again. I dreaded having to go to the meeting each week, and I dreaded seeing the impact that it had on Poppy.

Each Monday, I tried to start the day positively by showing Poppy that no matter what happened, she could get through it. However, I often came away exhausted from seeing little, or no, progress. The positivity was impossible to maintain.

It is hard to express your feelings or find the energy to ask questions when you are not at your best. That was me. Some Mondays, I wanted to stay in bed and pull the duvet over my head and roll over until Tuesday came. Other Mondays, I felt ready for the world, but it was soon zapped out of me. Some Mondays, I surprised myself and survived.

Another week had passed. Poppy's heart rate was slowly improving and was creeping into the 30s. Still very low, but it was heading in the right direction. Much to her disgust and annoyance, the meal plan was increased again. She was hysterical, and I couldn't calm her down. Nothing I could say or do made any impact on her. I was so thankful for the nurse who came over and sat with us, as she listened to Poppy. She was incredible and had such a brilliant way of calming her down. She even managed to get her to laugh. What a complete turnaround for a Monday.

It took many weeks for her heart to stabilise. Maybe it was naivety, but I thought it would only take a short time to get back to her normal self. How wrong I was.

I wished I had been given more information to prepare myself for what was ahead of us. I hadn't appreciated that recovery would take so long and that some people take years, some much less and some never recover.

Her body was responding well. She looked better, her colour had returned, and it was lovely to see that the harshness of her features had softened. I quickly learnt not to comment on her appearance as the ED would still tell her that she was fat and that everyone could see it.

I didn't know at the time, but Poppy took any opportunity to leave food, either by crumbling it onto the floor or hiding it up her sleeves. This depended on the staff member who sat with her, as some were more vigilant than others. She soon developed a list of people who allowed her to get away with things and those who challenged her on leaving food on her plate. Anything she could do to reduce her intake, no matter how small, helped to lessen the ED's thoughts.

Her heart rate needed to be a little higher. I wanted her home so much. I missed her.

Before she could come home, she had to eat several meals and snacks with me. That was a proud mum moment. Another key milestone for a parent to witness. It felt like seeing her walk for the first time. It sounds silly but it was a great first step. There were no disagreements, no negotiations and no crying. Wow! It hadn't been like that for so long.

They were pleased with her physical health and Poppy was able to come home. It felt surreal having her home, if only for a few hours. Then it was a night, a weekend and a week.

The weekend was one to remember as Mandy, the dog breeder, kindly allowed us to visit the puppies that were only a few weeks old, having heard what we were going through. Poppy couldn't stop smiling. She had a lot of lovely cuddles and chose which puppy we were to have. During the following few weeks she enjoyed visiting them and seeing them grow, and each time she got more excited about bringing ours home.

The only downside to the time she had at home was that she then found it difficult to adjust to being back on the ward, and her mood would plummet. She hated being there.

Poppy was finally discharged after thirteen weeks, and the puppy, Emmie, arrived four weeks later.

14

Back home

As much as I wanted Poppy home, I was worried that she might slip back into her old habits.

As much as I wanted to believe that having her at home meant everything was OK, the reality was that the hard work was just starting.

As much as I knew that we would make it, I was worried that I wouldn't be able to cope.

Despite what friends and family thought about Poppy being home, she was nowhere near being cured. That was where the battle was to commence. There would be only one winner, and it couldn't be the ED.

Being home meant that Poppy was around people who loved her and would support her, but it didn't make the fight easier. She would still have to fight the ED's thoughts, push against the rules and continue to work through her fears and established rituals.

She had been home for a week, and it didn't take long for me to feel alone in the fight.

Part of Poppy craved the routine of the ward, and part of her desperately wanted to be at home. She was in turmoil, craving some comfort in the vicious cycle she was trapped in.

It was subtle at first. She began chatting in the kitchen, just like old times, then came the odd questions here and there about meals, followed by negotiations of what she wanted to eat and want she didn't like anymore. Even though the anxiety had never gone around mealtimes, there was a noticeable increase. It began to feel that we had taken several steps backwards.

In a fight, your motivation and determination are sky-high, and you are ready to bring down your opponent. But each battle leaves you wounded and slowly, they chip away at you. The initial motivation slowly erodes until you no longer feel able to fight again.

That was how I was feeling more and more each day battling with the ED.

15

Bad morning, bad day

Poppy was still fearful of some foods and would do anything to reduce the amount she had of them.

This would involve crumbling food, dropping it on the floor, hiding it up her sleeves, smearing yoghurt, and storing food in her mouth as she waited for the right time to spit it out. Particularly when she was given food which she was intensely fearful of, such as butter, oil, cheese and chips.

She would become unrecognisable, with her face twisted in anger and bitterness, and her eyes full of venom towards me and the world.

She would shout and scream and do anything she could to avoid eating. You will have heard the saying, 'If looks could kill, I would be dead'. Well, I was the target.

It became too easy to write the whole day off. If the morning was off to a bad start, I assumed that the rest of the day would be the same. If I hadn't achieved anything that day, then why bother doing anything at all?

I was in a rut.

I convinced myself that scrolling through my phone was taking time out for myself. All it did was made me compare my life with others, but not in a good way.

I convinced myself that there was nothing I could do to change my day.

I convinced myself that that was my life now, whether I liked it or not.

All the battles, frustrations and stress were snowballing, and it was hard to see anything except that it was a bad day, a bad week or a bad month.

I was stuck.

26th October 2020

Dear Diary,

Oh! My head is splitting and it won't ease up. I know it is a tension headache. I have been having too many of them lately.

What am I supposed to say or do when she says that she is in so much pain? It was only 10 am but it was clear that she was struggling.

I couldn't stop my headache. I couldn't stop thinking about the mealtimes ahead.

Should I keep pushing forward with her fearful foods or do I go with the safer option to give her a break, and me too?

Deep down, I know the longer we delay tackling the fearful foods, the longer we are going to have to live with the ED and the longer she will be in pain. It is so hard seeing her like this.

People tell me to keep pushing forward and not to negotiate, but it is so difficult when she is in pieces. I know I should do this, but some days I choose to play it safe. I am exhausted and my head hurts too much for me to do anything else.

Maybe I am scared - but of what exactly?

Maybe I am scared that she will break - but she is breaking now.

Maybe I am scared that she will break even more - then what will happen to her?

16

Not just one monster, but two

It is hard to admit but, unfortunately, there were times when the only monster to show up was me. I cringe now, thinking about it.

People say that the best way is to be compassionate and distract her at mealtimes but when I was exhausted, feeling alone and broken, and faced with yet another meal that she wouldn't eat, the screaming started, and it came from me.

My inner monster was angry, frustrated and desperate. So I lost it. I said one of the worst things you can say.

"Why can't you just eat it? It's only mash. It was your favourite. This is silly, just eat it!"

The anger inside bubbled up and I wanted to scream and scream and not stop. I was so angry at myself, for the life we were missing, for the constant days of hopelessness, and for wanting to be freed from this life. I was angry at my daughter, angry at the lack of support from CAMHS and others who just didn't get it, and angry at the world. I was like a bottle of pop that had been shaken and exploded everywhere.

The pain afterwards and the distressed look on my daughter's face, were something that I couldn't forget. How was she going to eat after that? I had played into the ED's hands. I had made it even harder for her to eat. The overwhelming guilt added to how awful I felt about myself.

What had I done?

Why did I have to lose it?

Why did I shout?

Why didn't I just walk away?

The guilt and the sullen feeling in my tummy didn't leave me for a few days. I never had to discipline my daughter when she was growing up. She wasn't perfect, but I had not raised my voice to her before.

In moments like that, I felt helpless, alone, and guilt-ridden about what I should have done differently. Maybe I had pushed her too much, maybe I hadn't tried hard enough, and maybe I was causing her more distress. Those thoughts went on and on.

Some days I had no fight left. I was running on empty. I wanted to run away and let someone else take over. I asked for support with meal supervision but was declined, which made me feel even more alone. It was me and the monster doing battle. Right then, the monster was winning. On those days, when I couldn't face any more battles, my strength and resilience were depleted, so I chose safer foods and turned a blind eye to some of the compensatory behaviour.

Initially, I saw this as the ED winning and I was weak, but it was self-preservation as I put on my oxygen mask. If I gave up, then so would she. Pausing for a moment and taking a deep breath, helped me to keep fighting.

I recognised that letting my monster build, to the point of explosion, would hurt my daughter and give more power to the

ED. No more, not on my watch. It was time for me to listen and work with my inner monster. It could be my best friend or my biggest enemy. Right then, I needed a friend.

It took time to work out how to manage my emotions. I wasn't sure how, but I knew I had to. I wanted to be a better version of myself, not just for my daughter but for me.

It wasn't easy. Change isn't. It was easier to go back to the old ways rather than keep going forward and cement new ones.

I was learning to be kind to myself. I reminded myself that I was not going to get it right each time. It was OK to make mistakes. It didn't make me a bad person.

I then looked for something that had gone well and patted myself on the back for making it through another situation.

When it was either Poppy's or my monster's time, I could choose how I wanted to respond. I imagined pausing myself on the remote control. Moving away from the situation, taking a few deep breaths, and asking what version of myself did I want to be, gave me time to see things more clearly.

Putting myself in Poppy's shoes enabled me to have empathy. By showing that I understood her feelings when she was scared, the situation was often diffused.

17

Monsters and underwear

Do you remember the inner monster that I mentioned previously? It plays a big part in my life and can either be my friend or my foe. It is the loud, irritational quickly-fired-up monster with spiky skin, more commonly known as my inner critic. It is not cuddly and it definitely doesn't want to be stroked.

I want to introduce you to another friend of mine. This is the cute, adorable ball of fluff also known as my inner cheerleader, which is quietly spoken, adores logic and likes to make people happy.

The fluff ball believes in me and gives me confidence. It weighs situations up and helps me to see them with a clear perspective. Unfortunately, it is often overruled and drowned out by the spiky monster who pipes up and tells me that I am not good enough. It is agonisingly loud, proud and so convincing that I can't find a reason not to listen to it.

By screaming, jumping up and down, bringing up past failures and memories of shame and guilt, the spiky monster confirms the belief that I am not good enough, I can't do it and giving up is the only option. Somehow, it tries to convince me that it is looking out for me and has my back.

At one point, it all came to a head, with the spiky monster in overdrive. I couldn't see a way out of the daily nightmare. I was consumed with endless negative thoughts that life wouldn't change, and Poppy would never get better. This was going to be my life forever - in and out of hospitals, specialist units, appointments, disturbed sleep, distress of seeing continual self-harm injuries and worry that she would take her own life. She was getting worse, with little progress, as the thoughts in her head were continuing to bully and belittle her.

Hope had vanished. I had little freedom to be myself, even for a moment. I was in a black hole and I couldn't get out. I felt alone, empty and stuck and no one could help me. I began to think about ending my own life as it seemed to be the only way out.

But how could I do that to my children? They had already lost their dad. What would happen to them? Had my son not suffered enough? Was that the mum I wanted to be for my kids? Did I want to give in when times were tough? Was that the message I wanted to convey or did I want to show them how to face up to a tough life?

I couldn't go through with it. My kids needed me and I needed them.

I realised that those beliefs were keeping me in the role of the victim, making me think that life had done this and that I had no control over it. I was waiting for someone to rescue me and my daughter, but the only one that could do that was me. It was my choice to stay in the role or break free. Just like my daughter was being ruled by the monster in her head, I had listened too long and too attentively to the wrong voice. I was allowing the spiky monster to rule me by reinforcing my limiting beliefs. It was time to slay that monster and let the fluff ball be heard.

This is why I want to talk about underwear. Weird, I admit, but all will be revealed if you stay with me. Do you remember the underwear that kids used to have with the days of the week printed on them? What if, for bigger kids like you and me, the spiky monster and the fluffy ball had the power to display the beliefs we have about ourselves? Printed, plain to see, on our underwear. Small, delicate writing for the fluffy one and, yeah, you've guessed it, large bold writing that you can't ignore, for the spiky one.

'Not good enough'

'Not strong enough'

'Life's too hard'

'Why can't things work out for me?'

'Why is it always me?'

I listened too much to my spiky monster and wore its underwear every day. No matter how hard I tried, I couldn't seem to pull them off, as they clung to me. Those loud knickers had to go. So, I flung them as far as I could and pulled on the positive ones - out with the old and in with the new.

At first, they fitted well but then they began to feel uncomfortable. I wanted to take them off and put the old ones back on, because of the familiar feeling they offered. I had kept a few so, when life became hard, I would put them on. The print on them reinforced the belief that:

'I couldn't do it'

'It was too hard'

'Why bother trying?'

I was back to square one, listening to the wrong voice again. Wearing the same old underwear would give me the same old life, and I deserved better than that. We all deserve better than that. If we want a different life, then we must do things differently. We need to embrace change, invest in ourselves and get some new underwear.

Changing my underwear was the easy part. Keeping the old ones off and allowing the cheerleader (fluffy ball) to shine through was the difficult part.

How did I do it?

I began to change my perspective. It wasn't easy. It took time and practice, but it was worth it.

★ Focus on the now, not the past or the future

When I was stuck in the habit of focusing on what went wrong, I dreaded mealtimes and my daughter's reaction to them. Previously, I would have carried our battle scars, from all the times when she hadn't eaten enough, to each mealtime. As I reset my perspective and saw each meal as a new opportunity to get closer to my goal of freeing her, I was relieved of some of the pressure and able to see things in a different light.

★ My spiky monster

I used to think of my monster as being childlike and immature, not having learnt to manage its emotions, which could easily overflow into a tantrum if not de-escalated.

Having a negative focus, it would react spontaneously, with little or no consideration of another perspective. It certainly paid no regard to my cheerleader (the cute fluffy ball).

My perspective changed when I realised that emotions are neither good nor bad. They are a natural part of being human and can help me understand myself and situations. How I process and react to them is what matters.

When I felt angry, frustrated and scared, the spiky part of me would jump up and down. I used to think that the best way to deal with it was like dealing with a child having a tantrum, by ignoring and distracting it. But dismissing the feelings, and ignoring them, didn't make them go away; they kept piling up until I couldn't take it anymore. I didn't think I would ever say this, but the spiky monster needed to be heard.

Just like the uncomfortable underwear, it was time to replace my old thinking. Time to be free to feel. To be free to choose how to act, rather than feel the need to be strong, or the need to dismiss or hide the feelings.

My spiky monster has become a guide on how I am feeling 'at the moment', but not a determiner of who I am. Yes, the moment may be difficult and flooded with thoughts of my inadequacy, but it is just the moment, not the day, not the week, not the month, not the year and not my whole life. Moments do pass.

Our thoughts are formed by the opinions we hold about ourselves and the world around us. We believe them to be true, but they are not necessarily so. We give them a perspective of being either good, bad or neutral, based on our experiences. Often these beliefs were developed when we were young. That was some time ago for me, so they needed to be reset.

In this resetting process, I asked myself if a thought or belief had any truth to it and if it was going to help or stop me from becoming a better person. In that way, old uncomfortable beliefs, which were unhelpful and did not fit me anymore, were flung on the floor to make way for new ones. Fresh beliefs that the cute fluff ball could wear in high regard.

'I am good enough'

'I can do this'

Although this approach took time and practice, it produced a calmness in me. If I catch myself slipping back into my old ways, I rip them off and replace them with my new beliefs, just like I would if my underwear was no longer comfortable. Out with the old and in with the new.

★ My focus determined my feelings

I used to believe that I was weak and not good enough. As a result, I felt hopeless and labelled myself as one hell of a rubbish mum. No wonder I felt awful. Focusing on the wrong thoughts was disempowering and increased my sense of inadequacy.

My focus determined my feelings and, being in a negative state, I tended to focus on everything that went wrong.

I couldn't see any of the good things. With each tough day, I felt weaker and the underwear displayed that I was not good enough, not strong enough, not anything enough. I chose to listen to the spiky monster and not the fluff ball.

Even though changing my focus didn't remove the ED or the distress that Poppy was in, it did allow me to see the broader picture. I was able to see that there were some good moments, and there were times when we felt more connected. I had been focusing on all the bad. I began to focus on the good things which I loved about my life.

★ Celebrate the wins, no matter how small

As I focused on the wins, there were many things to celebrate: no hiding or spitting out food, no tipping out milk, and slowly increasing the time she was sitting still.

I would be ecstatic on the inside but not show joy outwardly, for fear of things going backwards. The inner cheerleader would dance and shout, "We did it, I knew we could", "We are bloody brilliant" and "Bring it on ED, bring it on."

In moments like that, I reminded myself that I had control over how I wanted to be. I could choose whether to react or respond to my inner monster. I could choose to be a better person today than I was yesterday. Those wins didn't have to be big, a win was a win!

Before going to bed, I would look at what had gone well, what made me smile and what had made me laugh that day or that week.

★ Go and grab your super underwear

When faced with challenges at mealtimes, knowing that the 'I am not strong enough' spiky monster was going to take control, I would use mantras that empowered me:

> **'Super underwear on'**
>
> **'I can do this'**
>
> **'I am strong enough'**

I stood like a superhero in my kitchen, with my hands on my hips, visualising myself pulling up my super underwear and seeing the 'SuperMum' logo, 'Who says I can't do this?' That empowered me and gave me the confidence to go and get the ED and do it for my daughter.

Food down, keep calm and keep pushing on. I even went as far as visualising my fluffy ball wearing super underwear, to give me that extra boost on those days when I needed it.

★ What does your underwear say about you?

Ask yourself each morning if you will choose underwear that proclaims a negative thought or belief. Or if you will fling them on the floor in a heap, never to be worn again, and choose ones that say:

> **'I am good enough'**
> **'I've got this'**
> **'I am capable'**
> **'I have achieved so much already'**
> **'This is only temporary'**
> **'I can do it'**

★ Be proud of who you are

What are you most proud of during this journey? It could be a million things, such as you made it through another day or another meal. You might be a single parent/carer getting through this on your own. You might be juggling work. You might have ended a relationship, passed your exams or moved house. You may have been there when a friend needed you. You should be proud of yourself, however big or small those achievements. Feeling good about myself has boosted my cute fluffy part - it practically glows. I want more of that.

★ We are not where we want to be yet

Yet - that is the keyword. This is a journey with lots of bumps, obstacles and U-turns but the destination remains unchanged. We need to reset the obstacles and see them, not as failures, but as opportunities for us to grow and develop.

★ Let yourself off the hook

If things are not going the way you want, remember that you are doing the best you can at this time. We all make mistakes and that's OK. We can learn from them. The past is in the past; today is now when we can be a better version of ourselves. Think about what you would say to a friend in a similar situation and be your own best friend.

18

How are you doing?

How are you doing? How are you really doing?

Just in case no one asks you today.

Just in case you are having a bad day.

Just in case you need a friend.

Whatever is going on for you today, you've got this.

It's OK if you are having a bad day, or a bad time.

I believe in you, I really do.

You can get through this.

You might not see that right now, but you can.

19

I did it!

14th November 2020

Dear Diary,

What a day!

She asked if she could have chips in the air fryer. I had a hunch that it wouldn't end well. I wasn't sure how I could best respond.

I was met with, "Why not? They taste nicer. Why can't I?"

It was difficult to know if it was her or the ED talking. Maybe it would have been easier to have said it was broken. She went from Defcon 5 to Defcon 1 at lightning speed.

"I'm so sick of my life," she screamed and ran upstairs.

I couldn't believe it, but I did it!

I didn't shout. I kept calm.

Thoughts were running around in my head. What if she hurt herself or worse? When do I go upstairs? Is it better to give her a few minutes or go with my instinct and run upstairs and say, "Yeah, you and me too!"

Too many negatives flooded through my mind and, for a few moments, I didn't see it getting any easier with Poppy. I craved dealing with 'normal' teenage behaviour, not that!

I remembered what I had told her, "Choose!"

I could choose how to react or respond. That helped to gain some focus. I reminded myself that she was hurting, scared and anxious.

I asked myself, "How would the better version of me want to act?"

I imagined putting on my 'be kind' underwear, pulling them up high and wearing them with pride.

I did it!

I felt in control, something I hadn't felt for such a long time.

My newfound calmness enabled me to connect with Poppy and explore how she was feeling. She described it as feeling weak from the endless battles. She felt that there was a brick wall in front of her stopping her recovery. She couldn't get past as it was too long, too wide and too tough to break through. With each step of progress, a slight crack appeared and sometimes a brick fell out. When that happened, she had a much-needed glimmer of hope that better days were coming.

But the hope only lasted for a moment. There was no rest from the relentless battles in her head, the endless food challenges, the mental tiredness, the pressure from school, and the agonising pain that soared through her body every day. She was full of anxiety from the moment she was awake until she went to bed. Feelings of overwhelming defeat erased any hope she had and she would see that the wall had returned, bigger and tougher.

She questioned herself, "How can I do this? How am I ever going to be free?"

When she was completely drained, she questioned her reason to live.

"Mum, I don't want you to fix it. I just want you to understand and hug me."

I felt my eyes welling up. My girl was in so much pain. I wanted to knock the wall down in one big almighty blow and I wanted to do it there and then for her, and for me. I wanted to fix it! As a parent, how can you not want to fix it? I struggled as I watched her struggle.

Maybe being there for her, listening to her, and letting her know that someone had her back, was helping to fix it.

I didn't see that at the time.

20

What will happen?

What will happen when I put food in front of you today?
My tummy will churn,
My head will start hurting in anticipation
Thinking about how to get you to eat

What will happen if I raise my voice and shout, "Just eat"?
It won't work
The pain across your face will be etched in my memory
The guilt and shame will be unbearable for me

What will happen if I reason, plead and cry with you?
It won't work
The guilt for you will be awful
Being a burden will be etched in your memory

What will happen if I put myself in your shoes?
I will see that you are scared, frightened and anxious
You feel like this so many times in the day
You keep holding on despite wanting to let go

I will see that you need me to be compassionate, calm and
there for you
I will see that you need me to distract you during and after
the meal

I will see that you need me to hold your hand and give you
a hug
I will see that you need me to ask, "What else can I do to
help you through?"

I saw the impact that mealtimes were having on her. No day
was the same. Sometimes she would be agitated, nauseous, and
struggling to breathe. On other days, she experienced
palpitations and there might have been tears, shouting,
headbanging and self-harm.

What was predictable was not knowing what each mealtime
would bring, how I would get through it, and how she would
get through it. My emotions could be a mixture of anger,
frustration, fear and hopelessness. A clear head was often
impossible.

Someone told me that I too was in a state of anxiety, not
just at mealtimes but throughout the day, probably every day.
Before then, I hadn't realised how anxious I had been.

My whole world revolved around Poppy and the ED. Every
day it consumed my thoughts and governed my actions. If I
wasn't thinking about it, I would be reading about it, talking
about it, and looking for solutions. I would have tried anything.
It sounds silly I know, but if someone had told me it would help
if I stood on one leg and said the word 'elephant' three times
backwards, I would have done it.

21

A game of battleships

I would love to tell you that it was all plain sailing after that, but the ED's grip was too strong and I continued to fight, trying to weaken its dominance in her life.

It was as if I was in a game of battleships. If you are not familiar with the game, each player hides five plastic ships and the goal is to sink your opponent's ships before they sink yours.

Each time Poppy would act upon her ED thoughts was a hit to one of my ships. Each conflict we had resembled the bombs being launched at each other. Some days the ED's hits came fast and furious and it felt as if every single one of my ships was sinking. As hard as I tried, I often struggled to find any of its ships. On other days, the game plan changed as we started levelling up and I was back in the running.

As in other games, there are different ways to win. Unknown to me in the beginning, the ED would use any way possible and didn't stick to the rules. I used to think that any calmness was a good sign, as the ED always had an undercurrent. It was either planning an attack or executing one and its focus remained solid, doing anything it could to win.

With each wrong move I made, I lost focus and momentum, and the ED used that as an opportunity to advance its attack, leaving me bruised and wounded. To beat the ED, I had to think smarter and had to put my energy into the right things.

When the game first started, I was energetic, confident and determined that the ED was going down. However, with each hit I experienced and each ship that sunk, my energy levels decreased further, to the point where it was barely visible. It was too easy to take the most comfortable pathway and bury my head in the sand. It was much better to pause, allow myself time to recharge and reset, to think outside the box and turn the tables. Surprising the ED was one of the greatest victories as it felt good having the upper hand.

All too often, that position didn't last long and I found myself fighting for survival yet again. I would often freeze, not knowing which direction to take. The strategy would be a distant memory, as I was too focused on where I was and close to giving up. In desperation, I would set off in a different direction, only to find that I had to do a complete U-turn as the ED had me cornered. Its attack often surprised me and I found myself unprepared, in danger of losing the game. There was only one thing I could do. I used my emergency flare and called for reinforcements. Sometimes help came quickly and other times I would be waiting and waiting for help.

Despite, at times, feeling that the attacks were relentless and all hope had gone, I came to realise that being behind didn't mean that I was going to lose. Learning from my losses was a great strategy to have, far better to take them in my stride, rather than waving the white flag and admitting defeat.

With the right support, I could develop a new improved game plan and, as a result, my energy levels, my resilience and my 'I can do this' underwear would go back on, and the game would recommence.

The goal of the game, to sink every ED ship, was back on my radar.

22

The ED was back, stronger than ever

Unfortunately, the ED had other ideas and the arguments got worse and the eating got tougher.

Every time she finished her snack or meal, it was as if her chair was on fire, and she stood up. I would ask her nicely to try and sit down. Often, she would greet this with a grunt, and say, "Give me a minute, Mum" or "I've been at school all day, it's so hard." Nothing had helped. The hospital had tried but the standing was still a problem.

Standing was a key indicator that things were spiralling out of control. I didn't want to see that happen again. She described it to me that the pain would spread throughout her entire body. It was agonising as it built in intensity and strength, and the only thing that helped was to move or stand. It didn't get rid of the pain but it took the edge off.

Things got so bad that sitting for two minutes after finishing her food was agonising. When days were tough, she stood for hours. It wasn't easy to tackle, so we worked on increasing the time before she stood. Her eyes would be fixed on the clock, willing the minutes to pass. As soon as they did, she was up like a jack-in-the-box, and nothing could stop her. It was frustrating, as no one was able to give us any ideas on how she could stop. I've tried distractions and hot water bottles, played songs with anything related to sitting down to make her laugh, pleading and raising my voice as I threatened to stop her going out for a walk. But nothing made a difference.

At times, I was too tired to fight as it seemed to cause more arguments and made me feel like a bad person. I knew I was the only one that must keep fighting her but it was every day, and not just once a day, it was multiple times. I wanted to quit and leave it to someone else to sort out.

I didn't know which way to turn as things were deteriorating quickly. I had to do something, so I googled for help and found several private specialist units. I wasn't sure how I could afford it but I was desperate for help. We had a CAMHS appointment in the New Year, which I clung on to with the hope that they could help. I poured everything out to them, how awful things were, how much things had deteriorated, how I couldn't cope, and how she needed help. Her stats showed signs that her body was struggling. They were not as bad as last time but they wanted to admit her that afternoon and asked for my permission.

I wasn't expecting that.

It was hard to stomach, hearing that Poppy needed to be admitted again. They were referring her to a Specialist Eating Disorder Unit (Tier 4) but warned us that it could be weeks before a bed became available.

I wanted the help, I wanted someone to fix her, and I wanted to say yes but I couldn't get the words out. I asked if she could stay at home until they found a bed. I was grasping at straws, as I didn't want her to go and I just wanted them to fix her immediately. She pleaded with me to not let them admit her. They were worried that if they didn't, she would be too unwell to take a bed when it became available.

I stepped out of the room for a moment to gather my thoughts and reached out to my brother for advice. He reiterated that if there were signs that her body was struggling then she needed to be admitted. I knew he was right. I needed to hear it from someone else, to help lessen the guilt of agreeing and seeing her crumble again. Poppy was adamant she didn't want to go but CAMHS advised us that they would apply to section her if she didn't agree to the admission.

They agreed that I could take her home for a few hours to say our goodbyes. We cried buckets on the way home. It felt strange walking into the house, not knowing how long it would be until she walked through the front door again. I went into mum-mode, collecting clothes and possessions, taking photos to help us both with the separation. We hugged each other for what seemed like ages, cherishing our last moments together. Watching her hug and play with our puppy restarted the tears; she would miss her dearly as we had got her so that she could help Poppy.

I drove slowly taking her back. We knew what was ahead of us as it was her second hospital admission. It was surreal walking onto the same ward with familiar faces greeting us with smiles of recognition. I had hoped that we wouldn't have to do it again. Memories of weekly meetings, with only one person able to visit and mealtimes behind curtains, all flooded back. Kissing her goodbye was gruelling.

Her mood instantly took a huge dip. She hated being there, texting me about how she was missing home, and how much she was struggling. Never really knowing how best to handle those messages, I returned to my old role of supporter and coach by sending her texts, photos and videos of the puppy, as well as motivational quotes and movie clips. Anything I could think of that might help.

Her texts became even more worrying. I had a huge impulse that I needed to see her again that day. There were thirty minutes left of visiting time. I rushed to get there, knowing that I would only be able to see her for a few minutes but it might be enough to make her smile.

Seeing her curled up in a ball was hard to stomach. It took her a little while to recognise who I was but her smile made it worthwhile. It was one of the biggest bear-hugs she had given and neither of us wanted to let the other go. I told her how much we all loved her and reminded her feelings would pass. I told her to hold on, and not to forget that I would always be there for her, and we would get through it together. I told her that we had done it before and we could do it again.

It was hard for her to be back in the hospital as it felt as if we were back at square one, but at least that time I knew what was ahead of us.

I tried to take each day and each moment as it came. And just as I said to Poppy, "We got through the last one, we can get through this too."

23

Specialist eating disorder unit

We were fortunate that, within three weeks, a Specialist Eating Disorder Unit Tier 4 bed was available and Poppy was admitted a few days later.

There were many uncertainties.

How long will she be there?

Will this help her?

What happens if this doesn't work, what then?

Leaving Poppy in the unit didn't get any easier. I kept telling myself that it was where she needed to be.

Due to Covid, there were several restrictions. Any new admissions were isolated from the other residents for ten days and visiting was only for an hour, once a week. It was not easy having to wait for ten days before seeing Poppy again. One hour once a week was hard to stomach, and the visits went by so quickly.

Poppy got used to handing her phone in at 8.30 each night, and she could live with a bedtime curfew of 10.00, but not with the thought of having to drink the Fortisips if her meals weren't finished.

It made a refreshing change not to be on hand to respond to her texts after 8.30. It meant that I could detach and sleep without feeling the need to support her.

She was placed on a 10-minute watch, but that didn't stop her from harming herself. Her self-esteem hit rock bottom. It didn't help that staff arranged to see her but then failed to do so. That was a regular occurrence and fed into the way Poppy felt about herself.

Mealtimes were difficult, even though she was eating everything and had done from day one, the guilt and shame were still there. It didn't help that she could see the other residents hiding food, and not eating. If all their meals were eaten during the week, they were allowed to have visiting time outside, which was something Poppy looked forward to. She missed her puppy, Emmie so much, and we brought her along on our visits. Poppy's face was a picture. They were both so happy to see each other. It gave her a much-needed boost to keep going.

Poppy was desperate to come home. It was hard to know if that was for the right reasons. The staff were concerned that, if she stayed much longer, she could go backwards, and they mentioned that sometimes they had to take a gamble and discharge sooner than normal. That was what they wanted to do with Poppy. She had been there for nearly eight weeks.

It was surreal picking her up. There was a mixture of excitement and trepidation about what was ahead of us. Would that be the last time that she would need specialist help?

All the advice that the unit gave I put in place straight away. I went back to the basics: not allowing her in the kitchen, no compromises, remaining seated for thirty minutes after food, and no toilet breaks during mealtimes.

On her first night home, I found her asleep on the floor. Having encouraged her back to bed, I again found her on the floor. This happened continually. Her self-worth had become so bad that she didn't feel worthy of sleeping in a bed, with any comfort, and it broke my heart to see her like that.

It was lovely having Poppy home, other than her sleeping on the floor. Things seemed better and her eating and standing had improved. But it didn't last.

Within a few days, it was clear that the fear around food had intensified, and the standing increased. It was as if she was too tired to keep up the pretence.

I still stuck to the basic rules that we had set. It was up to me.

It was up to me to keep her on the right road to recovery.

24

Hiding for cover

Mealtimes soon filled me with dread and anxiety. I never knew what version of Poppy I would get. There were times when she would punch herself and head-bang the wall. I detested that illness and the impact it had. I don't like disharmony. I am not keen on raised voices and I don't like confrontations. The ED ticked all those boxes.

Over time, I found myself gingerly putting the food on the table. I could feel the tension in my body. As if I had placed a bomb and the countdown had commenced. Sometimes the bomb would explode before it was placed on the table, and some days it could take 5, 20 or 60 seconds to trigger. I wanted to run away and hide for cover. I wanted to protect my daughter and myself from the blast, but I couldn't.

I am not a bomb expert, but CAMHS seemed to expect me to be. There was no formal bomb training, no bombproof clothing given for protection, and certainly no bomb disposal team available to pick up the pieces. I had to learn quickly on the job. I had to learn how to defuse the bomb or, at least, limit its impact during and after mealtimes. It could blow up at any moment. The number of casualties was unpredictable. There weren't many days when I made it out unscathed, especially not in the beginning. Despite my best intentions, distractions and cuddles, the bomb would still explode. Not a pretty sight. We were both left exhausted, ripped and shredded from the minefield we were in.

I would love to say that my bomb disposal skills are now redundant but, unfortunately, they are still required. Generally, my resilience to the explosion is better but there are still days when I want to hide for cover. I am only human. On those days, I remind myself that I must keep going, as my loved one is in there, in her minefield of constant grenades, with bombs in her head being thrown with nowhere for her to hide and there is little, or no, let-up. Pain is etched across her face and the scars weigh her down with each battle.

The fluffy cheerleader would be my best ally constantly repeating:

> 'We can get through this'
> 'We can do this'

Putting on 'we can do this' underwear came in handy. It gave me some bomb protection, as helped to reduce the blasts. Some days, the bomb didn't go off and she ate with no comments, and we made it out with no casualties. The only explosion would be the one within me, celebrating the win.

You too, might find that there are days when you feel battered and bruised and you want to seek shelter. Some days you may be ready and prepared to take it on but, on other days, you may be too worn down and would do anything to avoid a fight with the enemy, so you choose safer foods and a safer way to be. That is OK. It is OK if you need to sit down and cry or just take time for a rest. I had to do that many times and play it safe for my well-being. The battle would recommence when I was feeling stronger.

I was not retreating from the enemy. I was recharging and gaining more ammunition to bring it down.

Hold on to any moments where you managed to diffuse the bomb and prevent an explosion. Take a massive pat on the back, as you have been through so much and it will finally pay off.

Keep going through the minefield. Put your bombproof underwear on if you need to.

Keep going and look forward to enjoying the fireworks of excitement and joy when you both make it out alive.

It will be worth it.

You can do this!

We can do this!

25

Mum, the storm is coming

Mum, it's coming
Heavy grey storm clouds gather around her mood
Slowly arriving, without warning
Rain starts lashing down, forcing her to try and hide

Destructive winds slowly engulf her hope
Ripping out any last bit of joy and happiness
Pounding and bashing her strength and resilience
Unbearable pain lashing through her body

She changes direction
The storm follows
It seems to know where she is going
There is nowhere to hide

Exhausting her at her core
Fears spilling out of her tears
Wind intensifying, stripping her of her grip
Mum, help me, she cries

Hold on little girl, come closer
We are in it together. In the rain. Through the storm
I am here with you. Don't back down.
You can beat this illness

It may knock you to the ground, my brave girl
But you will rise again, you can get your life back
You can be whatever you want to be
You are strong, let's sit together and watch as the storm passes

Deep in the storm, the monster was pulling her one way and I was pulling her the other, to free her from its clutches. Back and forth we would pull, sometimes my grip would loosen and the monster's grip intensified, pulling her further out of my reach and I felt I was losing her. The more I tried to reach out to her, the more she slipped away into the distance.

I would desperately say, "Please, I really need you to eat. I need you to beat this. I need you to keep fighting. Don't let it win. You DO deserve a life full of happiness, but unfortunately, you have to go through the pain. Keep going, please keep eating. I love you so much, I really need you to beat this!"

There were times when I cried uncontrollably and pleaded for her to eat, to stop exercising, to stop listening to the monster and to start working towards being free.

She knows that I am always there for her. I might not have said or done the right thing at times, but I have been there, holding her hand throughout the many storms.

I have seen her broken, living in constant fear and doubt, defeated by the constant bombardment, bullying and noise from the monster. Her insecurities were deeply rooted and she believed that she didn't deserve happiness or to even breathe the same air as everyone else.

Sometimes the darkness became too much. She was overwhelmed with guilt and shame, and breathing was agonising.

No child should ever believe that they are worthless and cannot sleep with the comfort of a pillow or a mattress. My heart bled, seeing her lying on the floor with no duvet keeping her warm and no pillow comforting her head. Getting her to lie on the bed was met with rejection. Encouraging her to place her head on the pillow was met with squirms.

That illness eroded any self-compassion, self-love and self-belief that she had and there was no sign of her getting those back anytime soon.

Her time in the specialist unit added to her self-hatred, as she felt undeserving of the staff's care and attention.

Her bravery and courage were a credit to her. I am not sure I would have been as strong if I had a screaming voice in my head every day, ridiculing me.

Once the storm is over, a different person will emerge. There will be scars and battle wounds but each one will tell a story. A story of how the storm ripped her to pieces and how she overcame and rebuilt herself.

I know better days are coming. I have seen snippets of the old Poppy; a little smile and a little joy, maybe just a little, but it is there. I remember the date, 15th November 2021, when she said that that was the first time that she felt happy. I wanted to jump for joy but I played it cool. Well, if mums are ever cool when their children are teenagers. I am hoping that is the start of many happy moments to come. And I hope you will have those moments too.

To everyone going through this, whether it is you or your loved one, you are incredibly brave. I make no apologies for saying this again but to endure constant battles and to keep pushing through despite all the pain, that is bravery, that is strength, and I applaud you all. Please keep holding on through whatever storms and battles you face.

Keep holding your loved one's hand. It makes all the difference to know that they are not alone.

26

Longing for my life back

There had been a hard few days with no rest from the ED, endless arguments, and so many pushbacks.

I longed to eat a meal without any arguments, without any focus and without the presence of the ED.

I longed to go out with friends and forget about my troubles, even for a short time.

I longed for the ED's life to end, and a new one to commence.

27

Not another day!

Before the monster's invasion, I looked forward to spending time with the kids at the weekends. Working all week, family time was special to me, especially the weekends, as they would be filled with laughter, giggles, fun and often exploring the outdoors.

The joy of watching the kids running around, playing and being free, was one of the best feelings I had as a mum. Time was precious. Being a single parent, I had to work full-time and I cherished the time that we had together. It may sound silly, but I loved thanking them for a wonderful weekend.

Coffee and cake were part of our Saturday ritual and we all looked forward to that time. Poppy would have a large hot chocolate with lots of marshmallows and an iced muffin with Smarties on the top, and mine would be a cherry and coconut muffin. They saw it as a treat, but maybe that was the wrong message to give out, that sweet things were treats and not just food like everything else.

That was my way of making up for not being a 'perfect mum' who could take them to and from school or be there when they got home. On those rare days, when I could finish work early, I would pick them up from school. I loved it and it made me feel like every other mum picking their kids up from the playground.

It has been a long time since our weekends have been anything remotely like that. It is difficult to go out for food when your daughter won't eat anything unless it is on her meal plan.

Poppy was trapped by the monster in her head, and I was trapped in the house.

Often, we were both itching to go out. Days out had become a thing of the past, all activities were stopped as she was unable to walk far, trying to conserve energy to prevent weight loss. Leaving her alone in the house was not possible due to safety risks. I missed the life that we had.

No wonder the slogan on my underwear was 'not another day'.

> Not another day of stressful eating for both of us
>
> Not another day of seeing her in so much distress
>
> Not another day of worrying if she will self-harm or worse
>
> Not another day of being confined to the house
>
> Not another day of feeling stuck
>
> Not another day of feeling hopeless, alone, frightened for her future
>
> Not another day of having to pick up the pieces after each weighing appointment
>
> Not another day of hiding how broken I am

It was Groundhog Day. Nothing to look forward to, same thing, day in and day out.

I had no enthusiasm or interest in anything. Weekends were worse, as I would wake up feeling 'meh'. I didn't feel poorly but didn't feel great either. I couldn't put my finger on it, my get-up-and-go had gone. I just wanted to do nothing. I had lost my sparkle. I tried to pull myself out of it but couldn't. I was getting good at putting that brave face on but inside it was different. I was a crumbling mess.

No one saw it. People would say, "I don't know how you are doing it", "I don't know how you are keeping it together" and "I don't know how you are being so positive."

I didn't either. I held myself together, but only just.

I had no option but to hold on. I felt entrenched in quicksand. The more I struggled, the more I felt I was sinking deeper and faster, accompanied by pain, sadness, exhaustion and hopelessness. I wanted to be rescued and I wanted someone to rescue her. I was tired of struggling to get out, tired of trying to fix my daughter, and tired of seeing her in so much pain. I didn't know what to do. I was sinking deeper and deeper and nothing was working. I couldn't carry on like that. We couldn't carry on like that. My daughter needed me. I needed me. There was no one else that could do it for us. Her dad wasn't there to help and it was all up to me.

Counselling was a turning point. My counsellor was amazing, making me see things differently. It is easy to get stuck doing the same things, even though it is staring at you, it requires you to see it clearly to make the change. I used to see the scars from my past leave an imprint on me, such as my divorce, and losing my dad to cancer.

I could carry on using the past to hold me back and continue to wear the victim's underwear, with an 'I can't do it' attitude.

Or I could use it to motivate me, reset my thinking, and be my own rescuer. I could choose to see these as a reflection of the enormous strength I possessed.

And that is what I chose to do.

I had missed seeing the many achievements, progress and joy that we had had along the way. I had become too focused on the future and getting to the end goal of her being free. The counsellor helped me see the importance of being in the 'now', enjoying those little moments, and focusing on any wins that we had on the way. To celebrate how far we had come, no matter how little that was.

Poppy was often trapped in her quicksand thinking too. That triggered me into a 'fix-it' mode and I would try and distract her from her emotions. It didn't work. She was fighting against how she was feeling, making her sink further into the quicksand.

Just as in quicksand, the more you fight against it, the deeper you sink and then your instinct is to struggle more. It's a constant cycle. But the less you struggle and accept that is how you are feeling and that those feelings will pass, the quicker you can get out of the quicksand.

28

What's your why?

When you are having one of those days, or one of those weeks, when it is tough and things don't go to plan, and you can't see how you will get out of this, ask yourself, "Why am I doing this?"

My why is that I want to free my daughter from this illness. To get her life back so she can be whoever she wants to be and not dictated to by this illness.

Remembering my why helps me to gain time so that I can focus on what I am trying to achieve.

What helps you to remember your why?

29

Go with your gut instinct

The ED amazes me sometimes, but not in a good way.

We were attending puppy classes and Poppy took along her snack and milk. There was milk on the ground by the car. It seemed too much of a coincidence for it to be there but she was adamant that she hadn't spilt any and it wasn't hers.

It was hard to believe her. Part of me wanted to, but the other part knew that I couldn't. I would have put money on it that she had spilt it on purpose, and had used the small window of me getting the puppy out as an opportunity. I'm not sure why she thought I wouldn't have noticed the milk on the ground.

Sometimes it can be obvious to see what they have done and other times much harder to spot. The ED was so sneaky, some days I came out on top, yet, on others, I was way behind.

Just like with toddlers, you need to have eyes at the back of your head.

Something nagged at me and I wasn't sure what it was, but Poppy's body language seemed more uptight than normal, and she delayed having breakfast. I tasted her milk and my instincts were right. She had watered it down. At times like that, I had to reset my focus and watch her like a hawk.

You too may find that there are moments when you feel something is not right but you cannot put your finger on it. I bet you will be right most of the time.

Go with your gut instinct.

I wish I had done more of that.

30

Dodging doughnuts

Who knew that they could go so far?

Who knew that there was so much jam in one doughnut?

So many times, as a child, I bit into one and was met with the tiniest amount of strawberry jam. Not this time. Why was it not one of those times? I didn't know a doughnut could hold that much.

One half hit the wall, smearing sticky jam as it fell to the floor. The other came at me with full force, a quick duck-down and it zoomed right past, missing me by a fraction. That was a close call. Before I knew it, mine too was flying through the air, and the destination was as far away from her as possible.

It looked like a battlefield, except the red wasn't blood. It was jam, and the only casualties were the poor doughnuts. The only winner was the dog. Wow, what speed as she tried to scoop up as much as she could.

Who knew that they could splatter so far? Everywhere I looked, there was either jam, sugar, or bits of doughnut. Even the dog had sugar on her nose.

I couldn't hold it in any longer. I giggled and giggled. The more I looked around, the more I giggled. I looked across at Poppy and she was trying her hardest not to laugh.

I ran as quickly as I could after the dog to try and stop her from eating anymore and, as I did, I slipped on some jam and skidded along the floor. I couldn't stop laughing and my tummy ached. Poppy burst into a deep hearty laugh, which made me laugh even more. My sides hadn't ached that much in such a long time.

It was lovely to hear her laugh again. Maybe not the best way to relieve tension at mealtimes but Poppy did, in the end, manage to eat a doughnut. It was funny seeing the dog sit with so much attention after that, in the hope that another doughnut would be flung in her direction.

31

Pass the tissues

That familiar feeling of heaviness was back in my mind as the weekend had certainly taken its toll on me. I didn't realise how much. Trying to be the strong upbeat one was all-consuming. I don't know what happened. It hit me all at once. I felt anger, lots of it. I was angry at my life, angry at us not getting there yet, and angry at myself. Everything that wasn't right was reeling through my mind.

We had made great progress. CAMHS were happy with how things were going as there had been so many positives. I knew there would be some good and bad days, but I thought the worst was behind us. But seeing her new scars had mentally winded me. I felt I had let her down. I withdrew into a state of self-pity, nothing felt as if it was going my way. All my problems were raining down on me.

I wanted to give up again. I wanted to reduce the pressure in my head. I felt unwell, faint and weak. Everything was overwhelming, I wanted to shut down, to stop thinking.

I didn't want any more hardship.

I didn't want to have to worry when I went out and left her.

I didn't want to have to hide the knives and scissors for fear of her hurting herself.

That was when the monsters resurfaced. The spiky one wanted me to stay full of self-pity and kept reminding me of all the things that had gone wrong. The fluffy one? There was no sign of the fluffy one.

Feelings of panic resurfaced, awakening old wounds; the memories of not knowing if she would survive, re-tormenting me as if it was only yesterday.

Why had it gone so wrong so quickly? I didn't have any of my protective gear on as I wasn't prepared for the bumps. I had locked it away in the hope that I wouldn't need it for a while, but I was caught out and was paying the price. Closing my eyes, I was haunted by the memory of seeing her face tormented with pain, her eyes dead and robbed of any zest for life, and her body twisted to ease the discomfort of hating her body.

More worryingly, she had admitted that, for the first time in a long time, she didn't want to get better. She wanted to stay in the comfort of the ED. She tried to reassure me that she was working on getting her desire back, but she wasn't sure how. It was as if the illness had somehow taken a firmer hold on her in the short time that I hadn't been looking. She had relapsed before, was that a sign that it would happen again?

I searched for answers, methodically running through everything to find out where it had gone wrong, where I had gone wrong.

My eyes filled with tears and no amount of scenery on our walks helped. I cried quietly, hoping that she wouldn't notice. She is a super feeler. She picks up emotions and seems to carry them as if her own. Of course, she would notice.

In between the sobs, all the frustrations tumbled out, one after another. All that I wanted to do at that moment was to give up. But how could I? What would that look like? What would happen to her? Endless questions kept popping up. The fluffy one was working its way through, and the self-pity slowly disappeared as my curiosity increased, making me question.

> Do I want to give up?
>
> What about all the battles that we have fought and won, and the progress that we have made?
>
> Do I want to give in?
>
> Is that what I want?

"Come on, Mum," she calls, giving me a hug, "It will be OK," she said.

We seemed to have swapped roles; she was now the positive one. She used my advice, telling me to accept how I was feeling.

"Own it, Mum," she said.

I did.

"Visualise letting it all go, Mum, just like the clouds above us," she said.

I did.

It took a few attempts, but the heaviness lifted and I began to see things more clearly. I was overwhelmed. I can see that now. I hated seeing her hurting so much and it brought everything to a head.

She was right. I needed to stop fighting my emotions, acknowledge them and allow them to pass. It was only then that I was able to reflect on what was causing the overwhelm and ask myself, "What can I do to reduce the stress?"

Identifying and reframing can often help.

Looking at it from a different perspective, I saw how much she was struggling. The pressure building from her GCSEs, returning to school, as well as the pressure from her ED thoughts.

I just had to hold on and keep focussing on getting through the following few months. I was conscious that her way to cope with the strain of the GCSEs was to restrict her food intake and self-harm. I envisaged a few tough months ahead but was already feeling the pressure.

I began to see that I needed to live in the present. Not always easy to do. I took some deep breaths and saw the colourful sunset ahead of me that I had missed.

Poppy reminded me that there is always something good to come out of a situation, We might not see it straight away, or want to see it, but it is there.

She also reminded me that emotions pass and when they do we can see more clearly again, from a new perspective. I needed that reminder. That was something I had said many times to her, so maybe it was rubbing off.

It took me days to stop crying, I assumed I would feel better. I didn't.

My 'get up and go' had faded and was replaced with 'do it tomorrow'. I didn't notice the changes at first but soon it became obvious and morphed into 'can't be bothered', which became the new norm.

I would look around at the jobs that needed doing but I couldn't be bothered to do any of them. Psyching myself up to do anything seemed the only way. Everything felt like a chore.

Picking Poppy up from school, having a shower, getting dressed and even taking the dogs for a walk. Daily stuff went out of the window, and I didn't care if the house was a mess or if I hadn't showered for a few days. Nothing mattered.

I had to keep an eye on Poppy's eating and behaviour, but I was disengaged. I was there but I wasn't. I tried pulling myself out of it, but the crying wouldn't stop.

People have told me that when you are faced with struggles, it has to come out somewhere. Maybe this is me letting it all out. It has been such a relentless, tiresome, and energy-draining journey.

For nearly two years I have been the driving force to beat the ED, fighting to stay positive and strong. I have been there for her 24 hours a day, 7 days a week, answering, reassuring and comforting her, whether in person or by text. Doing anything I could to help her through the daily struggles, motivating her to not give up, and showing her that life is worth living. I have repeatedly bounced back like a coiled spring because my family needed me. Maybe the spring has become overstretched as I have pulled on it too much, with no rest. Now I cannot get back into shape and I am not of much use to anyone.

I kept saying to myself, "Come on, pull yourself out of this. Stop crying," but the sadness was firmly attached and I couldn't remove it. It was part of me and it was not going anywhere. Maybe the struggles of the last 18 months were catching up with me, and the fact that Poppy had not had a hospital admission for nearly a year meant my body was finally able to recognise and process all the hardships and emotional storms I had encountered.

Each day has been a fight. I had been telling myself that I could handle it, but I didn't feel like I could. I didn't have another parent to take over from me. I didn't have the option to give up or break down. I had tried to be strong and supportive, squashing my emotions, but it was unsustainable. I had reached the limit. Something had to give.

The mum Poppy saw wasn't what I wanted her to see, as I didn't want her to see me struggle. Why not? Why shouldn't she see that life can be tough? It can knock you down and sometimes keep knocking you down, but getting up is a sign of strength and courage. That is the parent I want my kids to see.

I love walking and have always enjoyed being outside, but I got to the stage where I couldn't even be bothered to go out for a walk. However, since it was not an option for Poppy to go out alone, I reluctantly went.

The ED governed Poppy's waking pace, and it meant a lot to me when she slowed down, choosing to push through the pain to reach out to me. It took me by surprise when she grabbed my hand. That spoke volumes as I could see that Poppy was still in there. That was better than any presents or flowers.

It was lovely when she held my hand and we walked together. Instead of me carrying her, she carried me. But I felt guilty about that since, as the parent, I should be the strong one, with her leaning on me, not the other way around. She reminded me to stop for a moment and be in the now. I paused for a few minutes and took in the surroundings. I saw the sunset and the beautiful blue clear sky, I heard the traffic in the distance and focused on our dog running back and forth to us. We hugged; only for a few minutes but it seemed longer. At that moment, I knew that everything was going to be OK. We would get through this as we had each other.

I can say it now, although I couldn't before, that I am grateful for the lovely friends that I have. One rang me out of the blue and asked how I was, which set me off and the tears restarted. I couldn't talk to her for a few minutes as no words would come out.

She was incredible. She got it, she got me. She told me that it was OK and that everything I had been through had built up. She made me see that I had pushed back my feelings and worries so that I could use my energy for Poppy, and that was my way of letting it all out.

She said, "Go with it. Listen to your body and don't beat yourself up for it." She advised me not to use the word 'should' as I needed to take time to heal. Her words felt right and made sense. I cried and cried, knowing that was what I needed to do.

I hoped that I'd feel better the next day, surely at some point I would. I needed to go to the shops, but I still couldn't be bothered. I thought about arranging to catch up with friends, but I couldn't be bothered. Instead, I chose to stay in the house and do nothing. Not a nice place to be in.

Maybe I needed to see my GP. I felt lost, not like myself at all.

I kept going back to the million-dollar question. How could I get Poppy to sit down and remain sitting?

32

Seeing clearly

Poppy was in a better place.

I should have been too but I wasn't. I still felt constrained, lost, and demotivated, with the 'I can't be bothered' attitude still difficult to shake off. My brain felt foggy and I had no drive. I was on autopilot with nothing to look forward to. I didn't know how to get out of it. I didn't know if I wanted to get out. Deep down, I knew I couldn't carry on like that and had to do something.

I arranged to have more counselling, which helped, as it gave me the opportunity to express my thoughts and feelings without judgement and gave me a different perspective.

My counsellor explained that, like Poppy, I had also become a prisoner of the ED. I had lost my freedom and happiness to the illness. I had allowed it to shape my days, my weeks and my life.

I was responsible for being in an ED loop every day. Everything I did, thought about or talked about, was somehow related to Poppy and her eating disorder. I was making it a huge part of my life; in fact, it was my whole life. From when I woke up until I went to bed, I was consumed with searching for ways to help or motivate her, anything to enable a 'lightbulb' moment.

It was a bittersweet moment when I was told this and it made so much sense.

It took a while for me to understand that, instead of being part of the solution, I was adding to the problem. I was so immersed in trying to fix the problem, that it was taking us further into the ED's world. I wasn't showing Poppy that life could be fun and worth living, and I certainly wasn't showing her that life went on. I had reinforced the ED's power and that it was acceptable for it to dominate our lives, that there was no fun to be had, and no rest from it. That wasn't true and it wasn't what we needed.

We needed a break from the ED. Action and consistent action were needed.

The old me would cancel going to the theatre with friends, for fear of leaving Poppy. My mum was around, so she wasn't on her own. It was time to recharge my batteries and have time away from the ED.

I had a fantastic time. I hadn't laughed like that in a long time. It was hard to relax completely and I couldn't resist checking in to make sure everything was OK. Being in the moment was a struggle, as it was too easy to fall into talking about Poppy. But the evening was about me having fun. It felt selfish but we need to be selfish sometimes, especially when we are up against it.

Hearing Poppy say that she wished she could get away from her ED thoughts made me feel guilty that I could, but it is better that I feel recharged than ground down and no good to anyone.

I cannot change what is in Poppy's mind, but I can change how I show up for her.

I wasn't setting a good example by not allowing myself time to have fun, laugh again and recharge. Life is for living, and we had both spent too long under the thumb of the ED. Maybe not to the same extent as Poppy, but I had allowed the ED to get the better of me and had given in.

The Christmas holidays would be on us soon. As good a time as ever to start changing my story.

33

Single again

Why does it keep happening to me? Why can't things work out for me?

Another relationship ended. Single again.

He muttered, "I can't see a future for us." Those words blew my world apart. It hit me like a big dense ball of sadness as it invaded my body and was accompanied by thoughts, "I'm not good enough," "There must be something wrong with me," and "What did I do wrong?" as they crashed through me in waves.

I went into a spiral, as I critically examined past failed relationships, which made it difficult to quiet the thoughts of not being good enough. My spiky monster was coming through loud and proud. The old comfy underwear was welded back on and no amount of pulling or positive thinking was going to prise them off.

Before I knew it, I was wallowing with 'I am a failure' clearly displayed on my underwear.

Failed yet another relationship.

Failed to protect my daughter from developing the illness.

Failed to beat the illness.

I languished in the thought, "It is me against the world, yet again. Just me against the ED." Self-doubt was magnified by, "I don't know if I can do this on my own again." The spiky monster was back in charge, and I didn't even give a backwards glance at what the fluffy one was saying,

I found myself feeling rubbish about wallowing, but it has its place. It helped me create self-awareness and accept where I was and how I was feeling. It wasn't a bad thing to acknowledge my feelings, so I permitted myself to wallow. However, it is too easy to get stuck in wallowing so I would say to myself, "Today, I am going to wallow, going to have some hippo time, and then I am going to move on."

I allowed my true feelings to come out, without judgement or trying to change them. Giving each one a word helped me recognise and accept them for what they were. It allowed me to recognise that they would pass.

When I first split up from the children's dad, I did some mega-wallowing. I didn't tell anyone that I was separated for some time as, for me, being single was something to be embarrassed about. It took me a while to admit it without cringing. Silly, I know, but it wasn't the life I wanted for me or my family. I perceived that people would pity me. Everywhere I looked, there were happy couples. Unknown to me at the time, I was grieving.

> I cried for the loss of my hopes and dreams as a couple and as a family.
>
> I cried for the loss of not having anyone to share my day with.

I cried for the loss of hugs which made everything alright, even for a moment.

A friend asked me what I got from the relationship. In the early ED days, he was a fantastic support, and I don't think I could have gotten through it without him. As time went on, he became more impatient with the recovery, less compassionate and more frustrated. He couldn't see the progress that Poppy was making. He expected recovery to be quicker and for her to get back to 'normal'.

I stopped sharing my day with him and confided in friends instead. I rarely spoke about how I was feeling, choosing to put on a brave face of positivity and resilience, but inside it was a different story.

I dreaded the ED's outbursts. Not just the impact on Poppy, but the additional pressure that I had to smooth things out so that no one could see how stuck she still was.

It wasn't helpful to hear what I should or shouldn't be doing, but he didn't seem to consider how exhausted and fed up I was. Some days, I barely survived and had no energy to fight back against the ED. Despite his good intentions, I felt scrutiny and judgement from him, as well as from CAMHS.

The ED monster had me where it wanted me. I was showing signs of weakness, my strength was wavering, and my confidence and resilience were at an all-time low. It was a great time to take back more control and that is what it did.

I was not on my game and didn't notice the behaviours slowly increasing, didn't notice Poppy hiding and spitting out food. Mealtimes were getting worse, and her standing was out of control. There was a definite backward direction. As soon as I was able to recognise it, I grabbed whatever strength I had and fought back. Wallowing time was over, it was time to get back out there and keep fighting.

34

Christmas time

Holidays have always been a special time for us as a family. The last few Christmases, instead of being full of magic, excitement and fun, have been full of ED rules, tears and sadness. Last year was unbearable as we were in the middle of a Covid lockdown and the ED was raging. Poppy's standing was out of control and things were looking bleak. This year, I was hopeful that the ED would at least be wearing its Santa hat.

We knew it was still going to be there, but she was more hopeful than last year that it was going to be a nicer Christmas. She had worked hard to get through another year. There had been many ups and downs but there were also some lovely times.

Having a perfect Christmas was another pressure Poppy put on herself to achieve. We had been working to change her mindset and understand that life doesn't have to be perfect, including Christmas. If plans don't work out as we want, that's OK and it doesn't mean that everything is ruined. We can still have a great time, with our focus on being together, with anything else as a bonus.

During the build-up to Christmas, she began to work on unleashing her inner Elf (sorry, I couldn't resist. I will stop the jokes as I can hear Poppy saying, "That's not funny, Mum"). She embraced the magic and fun of being a child again and made a list of things she wanted to do which were non-ED related. Dancing to a Christmas song, watching a Christmas movie, seeing Christmas lights, and visiting a Christmas market. Doing normal stuff made her feel more normal, less ruled by the ED, and gave her a bit of strength and determination to dismiss and fight off the ED's thoughts.

26th December 2021

Dear Diary,

We did it. She did it. We actually did it!

We had a lovely Christmas and the ED didn't ruin it. It was still there but so was the old Poppy. It was like old times, even though she was 15 she still giggled at the silly presents she has every year in her Christmas stocking.

Hearing her giggle was the best present I could have had and she enjoyed karate-kicking the wrapping paper which separated the rooms where the presents were kept.

Breakfast came and went with no problems. YES! Morning snack came and went with no problems. Another YES! Knowing what she was going to have helped her to eat.

It was awful timing that her brother had Covid and we couldn't go to my mums' for Christmas for fear of her catching it, but thank goodness for video calls. It wasn't the Christmas we hoped for but it was memorable and we made the best of it. It was fun, as we videoed through our lunch, watched the same movie, pulled crackers together, guessed the bad jokes and took turns to open presents. Poppy made us laugh when she unwrapped her presents, only to find one earring instead of a pair. I hadn't looked too closely at what I ordered and assumed there would be a pair. She took it well and made us all chuckle.

With my relationship in tatters, I couldn't shake the looming sadness as it had only been a few days since we had split up, but I still could hear his words, "I can't see a future together."

He wanted to give it another go, but I couldn't shake the uncertainty of us breaking up again. I was weary of his frustrations and snide comments and of feeling judged about Poppy's recovery.

I enjoyed the day. I had made the right choice, having time apart so that I can think about what I wanted to do. I loved seeing them smile and laugh and it gave me hope that better days were coming.

Maybe my relationship won't work out, but I know I will survive. I have been through so much and survived. I needed the kids to know that no matter what life throws at you, you can overcome it and do not have to be defined by what happens to you.

Christmas Day felt like old times. There was laughter and smiles all around; very different to the previous year. The ED rules were still there and things that Poppy would have previously eaten were noticed but not discussed. It was not the day to challenge any fear foods. We wanted to show her that we were there to support her and make the holiday time more enjoyable than the last one.

Holidays can be difficult times. They bring back memories of loved ones we have lost and remind us of difficult experiences. We can get into the trap of putting ourselves under pressure to make it special for others when being together is often enough.

Poppy wanted to share some tips which helped her:

- It helps to plan the meals as knowing what they are can reduce the anxiety
- Keep numbers small and talk to family members beforehand about subjects to avoid and what they can do to support you and your loved one
- Take the pressure off by not expecting the day to be perfect
- Remember that the ED journey is like a marathon or even an ultra-marathon. It is not a sprint, so it will take time to get there.

35

Mountain climbing

Poppy couldn't cope with her weight gain. She panicked when she saw her body changing and could no longer see her ribs or feel her spine.

I asked her to visualise climbing a mountain. Initially, there would be some excitement and anxiety about the journey ahead. Setting off with motivation and aspiration for the future, with a can-do attitude. A race to the top to enjoy success, freedom, beauty and peace. A long-awaited aspiration.

Initially, the incline is not noticeable as the path is smooth with a few minor ups and downs, but nothing to cause problems. Getting to the top is still in sight and the climbs are not too taxing.

You see the top of the mountain. You made it … but then you look out further and realise it wasn't the top of the mountain. Instantly, you feel deflated. However, you keep going, looking for the top, as you are desperate to get there. As time goes on, it takes a little more strength and the doubts start to creep in. You begin to ask yourself, "Can I do it? Can I get there?"

The harder climbs keep testing you, with twists and turns, and the weather conditions worsen your vision. The path ends suddenly ends, with no option but to turn around and find another way. You are lost and feel alone.

On one side there is a sheer cliff, and you must cling to the wall for safety, being constantly alert. Tiredness creeps in. Desperate for a break from the surrounding danger and fear, you crave comfort. "Keep going," you hear your family say, "You can do it!"

You encounter obstacle after obstacle, some easy to navigate, some requiring a fight. Some of these fights leave you with battle scars. Self-doubt nags at you continually and you feel weak, wanting to turn back as going forward is too painful and you can't do it anymore. You look around and can see no glimpse of progress, just more distance to travel. You groan and ask, "How much further?" You just want to get there now, and question, "Why can't it be easier? Why can't I wake up and be at the top and let this all be a dream?"

The constant challenges of steep ascent, tough terrain, and altitude get greater, making breathing an impossible task. Every part of your body is screaming and the pain is relentless. Frustration grows with each small step, offering little hope of the landscape changing, and the grand view of freedom seems a distant reality. You are on the verge of quitting but something in your head quietly whispers, "No. Keep going, keep pushing through. It will be worth it."

You take the plunge and push forward against the adversity and pain your body is screaming about. You somehow manage to find a reserve of energy and you push through the pain.

Reaching the summit is not for everyone, some falter and quit and never achieve the wonders at the top. Even the strongest people are tested to their limits. Despite the intense pain, self-doubt, uncertainties, and danger you faced, you did it.

You pushed through and you are now standing at the top. The place many people dream of. Such a magnificent accomplishment. You succeeded. This moment will be forever etched in your memory and inspire you during future adversity.

You can overcome whatever is in your path, just like the mountain you have climbed. You did it! The lessons learned can be shared with others to help them overcome their mountains.

You now feel on top of the world. The freedom you craved for so long. No longer held back by the rules in your head, or by fear. Everything is possible. You have no worries, just a great sense of triumph that you finally made it. Be proud of yourself. You deserve this feeling. Enjoy being free. Your family knew you could do it, and you did.

Glancing back as you climbed gave you the opportunity to celebrate how far you've already come, rather than focus on past mistakes or how far you still have to go. Breaking down into smaller and achievable climbs allowed you to stop and enjoy the scenery and not be in such a rush to get to the top that you miss all the beauty on the way.

When Poppy was in the hospital, she wouldn't have listened to this. She was too ingrained in the illness and her brain was starved. Only when her state of mind improved was she open to the idea that, despite recovery being painful, if she wanted a better life then the only way was through the pain.

Climbing can involve planning, preparation and therapy such as FBT (Family Based Therapy), which gives the foundation, skills and knowledge to enable us to climb and reach the top.

At times, I had to carry Poppy whilst waiting for her desire to change. Hearing her say that she no longer wanted the ED was a dream come true. But that was just the beginning. I had to remind her that every step she took was another one closer to the summit.

Maybe you can relate to this or maybe you are just setting off. Maybe your loved one is thinking about turning back. You are halfway there, wherever you are, so keep the summit in sight. It is a long journey, but it needs to be taken. Reaching the summit is there for each one of us.

You have the strength to get there. The view when you get to the top will be amazing but don't forget to pause as you climb and acknowledge your progress.

Keep focusing on how you will both feel when you get there and what you will scream out loud for all to hear. Holding my daughter's hand, I am going to shout, "You did it. I knew you could do it!"

I am also going to shout for all to hear, "We did it. I did it!"

We can stop the ED. You can stop the ED.

My dear reader, this isn't going to be easy, no one knows how big your mountain will be to climb, or how many times you will have to repeat the same rocky terrain. Keep the summit in mind. You can do it and it will be worth it when you get there.

Don't wait for your loved one to want to get better. Carry them, if need be, but start the journey and don't get off the mountain until you are at the top. The view at the summit is there for you.

Many times, I have felt cheated and defeated that we had climbed so high, only to have to start all over again. I wish that we could have jumped to the top and skipped past all the difficulties, the tears, the frustration and the pain that was ahead of us.

I look forward to when we are at the summit, enjoying the freedom. I feel that we are closer than we have ever been, and I know in my heart that we will get there.

Maybe not today, maybe not tomorrow, but we will get there sometime soon.

36

Be your own best friend

The harsh self-talk that Poppy experienced day in, and day out, had a negative impact on how she saw herself. She hated herself and how she looked, as well as the impact her illness had on others. She displayed kindness and compassion to others but could not love herself.

I asked Poppy to use the mantra, 'Be Your Own Best Friend'.

Be kinder to yourself, don't judge yourself and remember that you are doing your best.

You don't need to fight your feelings. Listen to your heart and make peace with your emotions.

Own your feelings and thoughts. Say aloud, "I feel angry, I feel sad." Remember that no emotion is good or bad. Let them happen, even when they feel uncomfortable. Watch as they leave and imagine them moving away on a conveyor belt or floating away on a cloud or balloon.

Best – be the best you can be with the situation you are given, you can choose how you react to things, and remind yourself that nothing is permanent.

Friend - what would you say to your best friend who is going through this? Will this still be important in a day, week, month or year? Would you extend compassion and care, reassuring them that they are doing their best?

I fell into the trap of relying too heavily on my feelings and thoughts and mistaking them for a reality which was not the truth. When I accepted them for what they were, I was able to see what was behind them and stop judging myself.

I asked myself:

> Is this thought or feeling realistic?
>
> What facts are there that support it?
>
> What would I say to a friend going through this?

Our feelings are not facts. Accepting and making peace with our emotions and worries can help create a sense of calmness.

It didn't come easy to Poppy as her default was to agree with the harshness of the ED. The 'Be your own best friend' reminder helped her recognise that she would get nowhere by going against herself.

37

Shhh!

4th January 2022

Dear Diary,

Dare I say it? I don't want to, just in case the bubble bursts.

Poppy is doing well. There I said it. Shhh!

She is eating better and mealtimes are not so stressful. It's lovely to sit down and eat without any arguments and negotiations. I hope this continues. Shhh!

Friends would regularly ask how Poppy was doing and, for so long, my response has been, "She is not doing great, but we will get there."

Over the last few weeks, there has been a step change. Her mood seems brighter, she is eating better and continues to challenge the fear of food. My new response is quietly spoken, "She is doing OK."

I feel a little anxious saying this. Some would think she has recovered, but others recognise that we are on a journey, and this can change at any point.

I hope that these ups continue long enough to show Poppy that life can be amazing, it can be full of opportunities and possibilities waiting to be grabbed.

It is reassuring to know that her weight has been stable for a while. She has a sense of happiness and is enjoying the different activities she is doing and seems to brighten up after meeting friends. Things are looking up.

I love my new sense of freedom, I am able to get out and meet friends and feel normal again.

The doubts creep in, questioning if this will last. I choose not to listen and choose to enjoy the moment.

It was inevitable that Poppy would get Covid. There was no idea what impact this would have on her weight and health. She was in bed for some days with a temperature and slept most of the time. This is unlike her and the rules the ED imposes on her ordinarily would not permit her to stay in bed, rest or sleep during the day.

As expected, the weight loss is significant, although CAMHS don't seem overly worried as her stats are normal and, in time, she will regain the weight loss.

38

Dear Diary

21st January 2022

Dear Diary,

She came downstairs yesterday and it hit me how much thinner she looked. She thinks she has gained weight, but whenever she thinks that it normally means she has lost weight. It is 4 days till she gets weighed. I do hope they will do something if I am right. I am getting scared again, as a year ago she was in the hospital. I don't want to have to go through that again.

The pain on her face is awful, she is drained from the pain of recovery, exhausted from the pressure of her upcoming school exams, and depleted by the bullying ED. She is struggling to eat and her appetite is diminishing due to the stress of the Mock Exams. I can feel that something is going to happen.

She has started holding food in her mouth again. I don't think it will make a big difference to her weight but I need to tackle it. I can't let the ED win.

I can't stop examining her from her head to her toes, trying to work out if she looks skinnier. Maybe I am imagining it.

I don't think I am.

She told me that she feels better than she has for a while. Can I believe her? I want to. I want to hear so badly that things are getting better for her.

Is this ever going to go away?

I hoped it was but right now I am not sure of anything.

I am so tired of watching her in so much pain.

I am just tired of it all.

Over the following few weeks, her weight continued to drop. CAMHS did nothing, other than check her physical observations. We were back to waiting for something to happen before they would do anything.

The better days that we had experienced seemed a distant memory. I was no longer able to leave Poppy, as her anxiety levels were high and she was struggling to cope.

It was hard to remain positive when I felt stuck in an impossible mission, trying to get to her quickly, to release her from the ED monster. But the closer I got, the further away she seemed. I was in a vicious cycle, going around in circles, with no end in sight. I felt that I had been teased, having been allowed a few snippets of good times together before they were painfully snatched away, with no idea of when the good days would return.

The tears started to form again. I knew I had to do something, but hope was fading.

My mind went into overdrive and sleep became more difficult. I found myself checking on Poppy in the middle of the night to make sure she was OK and not exercising.

The thoughts that we wouldn't get through this were colossal. As hard as I tried to be positive, I was really worried about her.

30th January 2022

Dear Diary,

I am having a really hard time right now. I can't stop crying.

Today, the pain in my head has been awful. The creases above my eyes feel permanently squinted to relieve some of the pressure. The thoughts of running away are getting stronger each day. Whilst I see snippets of me running away in my head, my feet are firmly glued to the floor and my body will not budge, but I don't know how much longer I can keep doing this.

I know I am not in a good place. I normally wake around 4 or 5 am, with no chance of getting back to sleep. My mind won't stop whirling with all the worries taking turns to show up. No amount of ignoring them will make them stop.

All I did this morning was cry, like yesterday and the day before. Someone has turned the tap on and I can't turn it off. Even thinking about crying makes me want to cry more. There is a big dark cloud over me and I can't shake it off. I have tried to think positive thoughts, what I am grateful for, but the cloud continues to hover. I have tried to push myself to keep busy and not pay it any attention, but I feel it there wherever I am, whatever I am doing. I looked for some sunshine, but I couldn't find any. I am not sure if I was really trying. I keep telling myself, "Shake it off, snap out of it," but no amount of talking to myself changes anything. It remains and the crying won't stop. There seems no hope that it will lift.

He was so thoughtful. He came over as he was worried about me, concerned that my messages were not making sense, which was unlike me.

I was overcome with awkwardness. I felt disengaged from him, from everyone, from everything.

It was nice seeing him. For the first time in a long time, I could tell him how I was feeling, how I had needed him at times to just hug me and tell me that it would all work out and that everything would be OK in the end. Maybe that wasn't the case, maybe I was deluding myself, but at times I needed to hear someone say to me, "You can do this. She will get there."

I am tired of keeping in all the frustrations, the worry and the anger; of slapping on a positive face, pretending I am OK, yet inside I am crumbling; of trying to convince him and myself that I was coping.

I was so relieved when I told him that I had struggled to share my day as I was worried about burdening him. I didn't want another person affected by the ED and had worked hard to limit the impact on others. Ironically, he was there for me today and we are not even together, which is confusing my head even more. Would it be that bad to give it another go? I am not capable of making any decisions right now.

39

Merry-go-round

I had to sleep. There wasn't a part of me that wasn't exhausted. I couldn't think clearly and I had no energy. It meant leaving Poppy unsupervised but I had no option. She was getting worse and I was scared for her. No matter how much I tried to get her back on track, she was undoing all the hard work.

I didn't know that she had restarted exercising, whenever she could, and hiding her food, to the point where she was barely eating anything at school. No wonder her weight continued to drop.

I flopped down on the settee. Nothing would have stirred me, not even a herd of elephants or a charging rhinoceros. I wouldn't have cared or raised an eyebrow.

That wasn't me. I had lost myself and forgotten who I was. Again, I had unknowingly allowed myself to be taken over by the ED monster and I didn't recognise, or like, who I had become. I saw someone, broken by all the fighting, who was bitter, angry, scared and defeated, with little to look forward to. A bit like a merry-go-round, going around each day, bringing the same battles, worries and outcomes, with no sign of anything changing and no clear way to get off.

Sometimes it would slow down enough for Poppy to feel that maybe that day was the day she could get off, only to find, at the last minute, that it would speed up and prevent her from getting off. Leaving her hopes dashed with the familiar feeling of Groundhog Day.

Poppy and I were on our own merry-go-rounds. She showed no sign of wanting to get off, whereas I really did and was looking for any way to get off the constant ride of turmoil.

I'm not sure how I managed to find the resilience which enabled me to get out of bed with a newfound determination that I was going to get off that merry-go-round. I began to reframe each new day, which helped me see that they don't have to be the same. It reminded me to look for what had gone well and to cherish our achievements.

It took time for me to feel less stuck and it didn't happen straight away. Then I noticed that we were laughing and giggling together. The arguments were less, and our time together was more enjoyable. It no longer felt like entrapment and the ride was beginning to slow down. Even though the ED was still there, I was able to enjoy the highs and learn to ride the lows and enjoy the fun and laughter we shared. The lows didn't last forever and they did pass.

I was able to think more clearly. Running through scenarios in my mind, if she had lost a significant amount of weight, then surely CAMHS would alter the meal plan. If not, it was up to me to do it. That filled me with dread, knowing that her fear response would be out of control. I didn't have any other options. I would need the bombproof armour to absorb the shouting, tears and deviance.

A friend once asked me, "If someone was holding a knife to your daughter's throat, what would you do? Would you fight to get them away from her or would you give up?" Of course, I would keep fighting but the difference was that the threat, which was putting her life at risk, was in her head.

I knew what I needed to do. I would have to ride it and pick up the pieces afterwards, so I grabbed a piece of paper and wrote:

> *Right, Emma, get your big-girl pants on tomorrow and start the day with a loud YES.*
>
> *Show Poppy that life is worth living. She can do it and so can you.*
>
> *Make Saturday the best flipping Saturday she has had for a long while.*
>
> *'Operation Let's make it a flipping fun weekend' starts tomorrow.*
>
> *Go for it, Emma. You've done it before, you can do it again with your big pants on!*
>
> *You are an amazing mum and ED warrior, let's show it you mean business!!!!*

It took me by surprise how motivated and great I felt as I wrote that. I had changed from feeling sorry for myself to feeling empowered and I loved it. The switch was incredible and I was ready for the day ahead. It was 'Underwear Time' and my big-girl pants were on. Wow! I loved my newfound energy levels. I was on fire and my motivation was out of this world.

The following morning, the first thing I did was listen to a motivational video which always gave me a boost. I couldn't wait for Poppy to come downstairs. I had covered the room with notes of encouragement and fairy lights twinkled around the room, with music gently playing in the background and several games ready to play.

She loved it. Wow, what a great start to the day. We can do this.

We needed that. The struggles were still there but we managed to ride them much better that day.

40

I feel so torn

Unfortunately, my newfound energy didn't last long. Poppy's birthday was only a few weeks away but she didn't want to celebrate.

I was torn.

I wanted to make it fun.

I wanted to show her that life was worth living.

I wanted to make it better than the hour we spent together the previous year in the specialist unit.

I didn't know if I should prepare any birthday celebrations, as it was looking like she might have to spend her 16th birthday in the hospital unless we could turn her eating around in time.

Despite trying different ways to get her to eat, I felt that I was fighting a battle I couldn't win. I was being pummelled by the ED, no amount of motivational videos were helping me to gain an advantage. I was fighting on my own, with no CAMHS support, whilst the ED was gaining territory each mealtime. Her strength had gone and there was no sign of it returning soon.

4th February 2022

Dear Diary

It's only a few weeks to her birthday. How I wish she was in a better place. But, oh no! Here we go again. I can't seem to move from the spot. Neither my body nor my brain wants to move. All energy has been zapped out of me.

I feel so torn, part of me wants to give up and the other part wants to celebrate her birthday. But I am exhausted.

She wants to die.

I don't know if I can go through another 19 months of this.

I wish I could fix it but I don't think I can.

I feel helpless and I am hurting for her.

This is not Poppy.

41

Michael Heppell and the power of YES!

More scars appearing on her body symbolised the intense pain she was in. Her way to cope is to self-harm and I would catch myself looking at the scars when I accidentally brushed against her. Instead of feeling her smooth skin, it was rough and ragged. It hurt me and I wished they would disappear without a trace but I knew that there would be more to see next time.

It pained me to see that my little girl had cut herself to relieve her pain. New wounds spiralled thoughts of failing her as a mum. It was my job to protect her and keep her safe. But the evidence was plain to see that I couldn't do it.

Every time she hit herself or headbutted the wall, I felt like I had been slapped too. The spiky monster would grab my emotions and swing them at me, then I would use them to beat myself up, saying, "I have failed miserably. I am not a good mum." I saw it as my failure to support her in her distress. My failure label was getting bigger each time, weighing me down until I believed it was true.

It may sound absurd that labelling myself as a failure gave me some comfort in my unstable life. Ironically, I was setting myself up to fail and predicting my results before I had even taken the next step. The belief was so ingrained that I saw myself as someone who gives up and doesn't succeed, someone who is a failure.

I particularly felt a failure at mealtimes. When things escalated at the dinner table, I wanted to grab my keys and run away. I perceived that as being weak, but we all can get to a level where we need to take some time out for ourselves, to recharge so that we can fight another day.

Was I a failure? Should I label myself as one? Who says I was failing?

I was the one telling myself that, no one else.

How could I be failing?

I was saving my daughter from living a life ruled by the monster in her head. Every mouthful she ate, and every behaviour squashed, was one step more to free her from the controlled, belittling world she was in. That was not a sign of failure. That was a determined mum who would not stop until her daughter was free.

No journey is smooth. We know that the ED is relentless, up and down, never in a straight line. How we see things is not always how they are. Failure is not a full stop, it's a comma. We were not there yet. It took me a while to recognise that this was not me being weak or a failure. This was me needing help and self-care, and me needing to be kinder to myself.

I found it hard to cope every day with no let-up, working out what I should say, what I could do to make things easier, but sometimes, you just can't. On one occasion, her anxiety and fear levels were through the roof, nothing I was saying was working, things were escalating and food was thrown across the table as she refused to eat it. I had run out of ideas to get her to sit at the table, let alone pick up her cutlery. I resorted to taking her to my mum's to eat there. The change of scenery worked as she was able to calm down, and so was I.

When things escalated with no one around, I would have to keep an eye on her, using my phone video, whilst distancing myself to have time out. It felt as if I was spying on her but she knew that it was to safeguard her from being tempted to remove or hide food. It wasn't something that we did regularly, but it had its place when needed.

Every parent I know has lost their patience. We haven't meant to as we intended to keep calm. When this happened, I would review what I said, what I did, what I should have said, and what I should have done. I would examine and re-examine if I raised my voice, even for a minute, and if I wasn't as compassionate as I thought I should have been. No wonder I was finding it hard. I was not only fighting the ED but also fighting my thoughts, beliefs and the societal pressure of how a parent should be. It was important for me to remember that I don't look at my friends differently when they say they have shouted, so why should I look at myself differently?

I am very fortunate to have a close bond with my daughter and son, and, surprisingly, one of the good things that has come out of this, is that we are all closer.

Confession time, and I feel vulnerable admitting this, for fear of being judged as a 'bad parent'. It is hard to admit that I have already labelled myself as one, but to have it confirmed by others is even more daunting. This was an enormous worry for me, adding to my imposter parent syndrome, with the nagging doubt that, if people could see that I was not a 'perfect mum', she might be taken from me. I put so much pressure on myself to live up to my ideal of what I thought a 'good parent' should look like, and if I didn't, then I was a rotten mum. I worried on the few occasions that I did shout that it might cause her some harm. As a parent that is never your intention. You always want the best for your children but it is not easy being a parent, especially an ED parent.

It had been a hard week and the shouting, screaming, and adamant refusal to eat just topped it off. I couldn't take any more. What I should have said to her went out the window as I was too drained. I wanted a meal where there was no fear and drama, just peace and quiet, like in the old days.

I lost it. I saw not just red but every colour as they flashed through me. The anger and frustrations overtook my logic and I couldn't see or think clearly. The last few weeks and months all spilt out. I was weakened by all the times when I had to fight to keep myself strong and motivated, and my thick skin intact to deflect the looks, the grief, and the comments from penetrating my resilience. I was worn out and couldn't get the words out to encourage her to sit down or to eat. I wanted to scream at her, "Just eat." I knew that wasn't going to work, but I couldn't stop myself. I shouted, she shouted, I shouted back and so did she. I had reached a point, and the snack got it as I threw it in the bin. It wasn't the best move that I had made, shouting at her. Why did I think that would help? I knew it was the wrong thing to do. I had played into the hands of the ED. It had won and I admitted defeat.

The elephant in the room was still there. How on earth was I going to get her to eat now? We were both too upset. It wasn't her fault that I had lost it. I had to turn it around somehow and get her to eat. And I did, or rather, she did. I'm not quite sure how she did it but I suspect it was that she knew she wouldn't have been allowed to go to bed without eating. Thankfully, we were both calmer the second time around and more hugs followed that night.

Nevertheless, I was mortified. I felt that I had failed her big time, as I had done the one thing that I shouldn't have done by shouting at her. When a person is scared and has extreme fear, should someone shout at them?

I cried inconsolably and didn't know what to do, as the guilt, shame and anger with myself were plain to see. I am not sure who made the first move, but we hugged each other closely, both of us crying. I apologised profusely and opened up to her about my struggles. Thank goodness she understood. I was worried that I had made it worse.

Maybe, just like me, you have been advised on what you should do and say, and the importance of looking after yourself and putting your oxygen mask on first so that you can look after others. But it is incredibly hard to find the time or justify finding the time, and your circumstances can make it even harder such as when you are a single parent, or your partner isn't supporting you in the way you need them to. You might not be just supporting one child, but your whole family and finding time for yourself is impossible.

I thought I needed to be a 'Super Mum' with infinite strength, a never-ending supply of energy and unlimited resilience. I never considered my needs as a priority as everybody else's came first. No one can survive a constant battle with no rest. No wonder I lost it. There comes a point where we can't take anymore, and something must give.

No one advises what to do when you reach the point of no return. No one talks about it.

Anger can take us by surprise. Despite my best intentions, and letting her words fall on the floor, there have been odd occasions when some unkind words would spill out. Said in the heat of the moment, they weren't meant and I was instantly remorseful. Apologising with lots of hugs and 'love you loads' went a long way for us. It was the same for her, as I knew she didn't mean it; it was her way of coping with the ED in her head. I never loved her any less and didn't look at her differently. We both recognised that these were challenging times and we weren't going to get it right all the time, but we knew that our hearts were in the right place and our love for each other was never under question.

Apologising to her helped but it didn't rid me of the guilt and shame. Being a people-pleaser, situations in which I feel that I have upset the other person, don't sit well with me. I would carry the 'I am a rubbish parent' label around for days. It made my resolve stronger to get my emotions under control as I could control how I reacted and responded.

It needs saying, and maybe I need to hear it one more time, that we will all have times when we are stressed, frustrated, maybe even angry, and we might say unkind words that we didn't mean. That doesn't mean that we are bad people, bad parents, or bad friends. We are human, we are not robots. We all have our triggers and, when faced with these, it can be hard and sometimes it feels impossible to manage our emotions. Some of us will be stressed by financial worries, whilst others will be stressed by screaming children or seeing their loved ones slip away in front of their eyes.

We can't always control what happens to us or how our loved ones react.

Sharing my day and talking through my emotions and frustrations to a friend who would listen, without fear of judgement, helped to lift my mood. Often, we would end up laughing. Have you heard the saying, 'if you don't laugh, you cry'? That was us.

It may seem silly to some, but I was embarrassed to ask for help, thinking it was a sign of weakness or that others might see it as that. That is not true. It is brave and the right thing to do. I hope that if you, or anyone that you know, are struggling, for whatever reason, you would consider seeking help.

I can't deny that it hurts, and has often made me cry when Poppy has raised her voice at me, escalating with each request to put more cereal in her bowl or put more butter on the sandwich. CAMHS had told me to give her more control over her eating, but the constant arguments were draining.

It must hurt her too when I raise my voice. I say the usual thing, that I will not shout next time, but sometimes I find myself in the same cycle, doing the same thing.

A good friend of mine, Michael Heppell, helped me to see things in a different way and the power of Yes!

We tend to think of anger as a negative emotion, but if we could see it in a more positive light, it would empower us to change a situation. Redirecting my anger at the ED summoned up the strength that I only dreamt of. With each win, no matter how small or infrequent, I would fist-pump the air whilst silently, but strongly, mouthing, "YES!" That encouraged me to keep going, to keep overpowering the ED monster.

For an extra boost, I would say the word again, louder, and my fist punches got more exaggerated. I would imagine that I had achieved the impossible and fist-pump the air with both arms. Have a go with me, and let's shout YES three times, out loud. You might have heard, 'fake it till you make it' so let's say it like you mean it.

Yes

Yes!!

YES!!!!!!!!

If, like me, your first attempt might have been rubbish. I said it too fast, too quietly and without any emphasis. I felt daft and hoped that no one had seen me. If you embraced it, well done, that's brilliant. Have another go and see if you can get someone to do it with you.

I still find it slightly uncomfortable, but it feels great afterwards. Try it with me again, and let's really get into it. Imagine that you are feeling on top of the world. You are ecstatic, and that feeling is building. You have done it, you have achieved everything that you wanted to.

Now, let's shout this from the rooftops, and let's blow the rooftops off. Let's celebrate and show the world how amazing we really are!

Yes

Yes!!

YES!!!!!!!!

It may take a few attempts for you to feel comfortable. Maybe try when no one is in the house, or when you go for a walk and no one is around. Then shout it out at the top of your voice. Feel it, see it and go for it.

It doesn't have to be the word 'Yes'. It could be anything that empowers you, that makes you feel absolutely amazing.

When Poppy was struggling, we would replace the word 'Yes' with 'Fight'. We would both shout out, "Fight, fight and fight," and it seemed to work better on those days.

I promise you, my dear friend, that I have not lost it. It can feel great, so give it a go. You might be surprised.

Practice is the key. I kept practising and getting Poppy to keep saying, "Yes, Yes, YES," even on those days when we were feeling good, and things were going OK. It is surprising how pumped up it can make you feel for the morning or the day ahead.

Sitting down, first thing, with my work laptop, yes, you've guessed, I would even shout it aloud then and it felt better for the morning ahead. Keep practising, and when the difficult days come, and you are not feeling great, it will be easier to do. It might seem unthinkable to do it then, but you need to shout it from the rooftops, especially on those days. It didn't change what I was going through or rid my loved one of the ED, but it helped lift my mood.

As simple as shouting three words is, it can change your state and help you see that you can do this. Anything is possible.

My dear friend, I know you can get through this. I have been there many times when I felt awful and wanted someone to make it go away. But no one was going to rescue us; it was up to us. I had the power in me. I just needed to see that I was the driving force for my feelings.

You may need to do this a few times before you start to feel it. Don't worry if your family and friends think that you are bonkers. Who cares? Maybe get them to do it with you, it will be fun watching them have a go. But do it for yourself.

I know that you care very deeply and I am here to remind you that you can get through this. Let's start by changing what we say to ourselves and start saying YES to you getting through this, YES to you beating the ED, and YES to you, the amazing warrior that you are. YES!!!

42

Fun, what's that again?

It took a friend to point out that I was still doing it.

Everything I was doing was with Poppy in mind. The courses I enrolled in, the pathway to becoming an emotional therapist/coach; yeah, you've guessed it, all with her in mind. I was always thinking, "I am going to try that, it might help her." My spare time was taken up with reading, talking to friends, watching videos and scrolling through social media; all ED-related.

I rarely thought about myself. I lost who I was and became an ED mum. It was a very important role to help my daughter beat the illness but I was buried under the struggle.

Fun? I'm not sure what fun means. There hasn't been much fun in my life in the last 19 months. It's not to say that there haven't been moments when we have laughed, but there have been more tears than laughter. I had forgotten to have fun.

I was asked what I did for fun. I couldn't answer, I didn't feel I had much fun in my life. I had the odd time out with friends which I loved but that was it, there was nothing to look forward to. When times are tough, you need more fun than ever.

Children have a wonderful enthusiasm for learning and a zest for life. My two have given me the opportunity to look at life through a different lens, to see things from a child's perspective. I love that they bring out my silly, carefree, childlike fun side. Letting them put makeup on me, playing games, watching videos, and reading endless stories at bedtime were great moments. As they got older, life got in the way and we spent less time together and more time on electronic devices.

I looked back fondly at those times when Poppy and I would sit for hours in the hospital, playing games to distract from her ED thoughts. When she first came home, the dining table was full of games which we played regularly, but as the pressures of school and work increased, those times decreased until they eventually stopped. We were soon back to our old ways, often too frazzled to think about playing a game, although that was even more reason to do it.

One thing which helped was setting a reminder. It may sound sad, but it gave me the much-needed kick-start to guard family time. It gave us time to be silly and carefree, which is a must on this journey.

43

Trying to be a perfect mum

In my heart, I always wanted to be a perfect mum.

I thought I wanted to be perfect for my kids, but it was me who craved perfection. My kids never expected perfection from me.

I had tried for many years to achieve the impossible. I was never a hundred per cent sure what a perfect mum looked like, but I had a nagging doubt that I wasn't close.

As a single parent, there was no option for me to not work, however, it brought guilt of not being there enough, to take or pick them up from school. I would always take them to school on the first day of the new year's term. I needed to do that to make me feel that I had started the year right for them. Silly I know, but I did that every year while they were at primary and junior schools. It made me feel better for not being there all the time, like the other mums.

Only recently have I realised that I have been putting myself under pressure to be perfect, not just with my children, but with friends, relationships, work and everything I do. If I wasn't the best I could be, I had a sense of failure that was difficult to shift.

Why did I need to put myself under that pressure? There seems to be an expectation for us to be perfect parents. Comparing ourselves with others seems to be the norm. I have done this and I suspect you may have as well. When you look at other parents in the playground, at work or scrolling through social media and they look as if they have got it together. We ask ourselves, "How can they make it look so easy?"

On social media, we see lots of photos of smiling families, happy children and great holidays, but not many of the reality of parental struggles, squabbling children, or parents frazzled by lack of sleep. I can't help feeling that there is a sense of criticism if you lose your temper or if your children misbehave. It is easy to forget that we only see a snapshot. They are probably just like you and me, trying to do the best they can to be a perfect parent.

We can try too hard. I tried to be both parents to somehow fill the void of losing their dad. Poppy missed his cuddles and his bristly stubble that would tickle and make her smile. She missed asking him question after question about how the world worked. If I could have grown some facial stubble, I would have done it; anything to relieve the pain. I can see now that she needed to go through it and trying to make up for it wouldn't have lessened her pain. It just made me feel less helpless.

As a mum, living with the ED every day became a mixture of trying to get it right, not messing up and not saying the wrong thing. I always had good intentions to be compassionate, caring, calm and full of empathy. It was hard to not give a reaction when trying to ignore her words, and the moaning and shouting. I think I could have coped better if it only happened once or twice a week or even once a day, but it was every mealtime, up to six times a day. Groundhog Day at its best. The same distress, the same level of exhaustion and the same feelings of guilt and shame for not being a good enough parent. The stress of each meal would be carried to the next, and the next, taking a further bite of energy and strength each time. Deeper and deeper, I would feel overwhelmed with dread and failure as I couldn't manage our distress.

I had to work on the feelings of not being a good enough mum and the guilt of getting things wrong.

One lesson I learnt, early on, was to go with your instinct. I had often seen signs but had chosen to ignore them. Now, when I have a hunch, I go with it and am usually right. The strain is easy to read on her face, as well as knowing that the ED is sneaky and will do anything to keep her in the mindset of restricting, so I am aware that she is likely to revert to this and compulsive exercise.

Once I had a suspicion that she was restricting her food. The Mock Exams were close and I could see the pressure she was under. When I asked if she had eaten all the food, I didn't believe her when she said yes, so I went to check. Confirming my hunch, she rushed to beat me to the bin. She had thrown some of the food out. I had even stood next to her when she was preparing it, so I'm not sure how I missed it but looking away for a few seconds creates an opportunity. The fact that she had cleared up after herself was a flashing warning sign.

Another time when I asked her if she had used up all the chicken. I didn't believe it when she said yes and checked the bin. There it was; not a huge amount but it was a sure sign that she was struggling and I needed to watch more closely.

I struggled to spot the lies. That was a complete shock as it was so out of character for her. As a child, she was never in trouble and had never lied, so it was hard to believe that she would lie to me. So I ignored my instinct when it told me something wasn't right. Why would I even consider it? It wasn't something that I was expecting she would do. The lies became a daily thing, and it was hard to know what was true and what wasn't. I had to remind myself that it was due to her illness, not my parenting skills. I had to be on my toes. I couldn't believe everything she said, especially when it was related to food or exercise.

I loved hearing about other families who succeeded and beat the illness, as it gave me hope that recovery is possible. I spent too much time scrolling through social media, listening to how other families were suffering. Sometimes it kicked more resolve into me but, other times, it deflated me further. I found myself too immersed in that world, and have learnt to have some time away from it, even if just for a short time.

There was a part of me that couldn't help wondering, "What am I doing wrong? What if I am making it harder for her? Should I be doing more to help?" Perfectionism was creeping in again.

I worry too much about what other people think. There are still some friends, not close but the ones we don't see very often and catch up with a few times in the year. They do not know what we have gone through, not necessarily because they will judge but mostly to protect Poppy. I don't want many people to know as there is still a stigma about having a mental illness, and she has enough to contend with. It is not nice being judged or feeling judged. As a society, we have come a long way but the stigma is still there, and it's Poppy's story to tell, not mine.

If I was affected directly then I could approach it differently. Poppy might, at some point in her life, want to be free of this illness, and not be reminded about it. Therefore, I have decided to write this anonymously to protect her and give her the choice to tell her story when and if she wants to.

I have allowed myself to feel like a rubbish parent too often. As a single parent, it is difficult to balance my time between Poppy and Jordan. Throwing the ED into the mix makes it harder and I feel for Jordan when I spend so much time with Poppy. I am grateful that he supports us both but I need to keep working on the balance; not just for him, but for me too.

I have allowed self-doubt to creep in. I prefer to listen to others' advice rather than voice what I believe. When I found the courage to speak, and my concerns were not taken seriously, it knocked my self-esteem, magnifying my feelings of being an overprotective, overreacting and not a good-enough parent. I had to develop a thick skin and shrug off the dismissals. I knew my daughter and I knew when something wasn't right better than anyone. Sometimes you must keep beating that drum until someone listens. Putting on my big pants came in handy for those occasions.

Worrying about what people thought about me was ingrained in me and, being a people pleaser, I would overanalyse what I said, (what I didn't say), what I should have done, (what I shouldn't have done). I questioned everything as I wasn't confident in my decisions, and it was made worse by supporting Poppy and no one listening to us. My daughter's life was reliant on me getting it right.

I hadn't realised for years that I wasn't really being me, and I felt lost in life as a result. I never felt confident in my decisions, and I continued to question everything I said and did. I had been too busy trying to be perfect, to fit in, to be liked and to be what I thought people wanted me to be.

One thing I was sure of was that I was doing the best I could for my family at the time. Every. Single. Time. Yes, I made mistakes, but never intentionally would set out to hurt anyone. This helped me in moments when I felt not good enough: did I intentionally miss a snack or say or do the wrong thing? Of course not. You might have experienced something similar where you wished or could have done things differently. Did you intentionally want to make it hurt them, or make it harder for them? I am sure that the answer would be, "No." Just like me, you would have done the best you could at the time, with what you knew and what tools or advice you had.

The ED is a bully. My inner critic (the spiky monster) can be a bit of a bully at times and, like Poppy, I have the choice to either listen to it (whilst appreciating that it is incredibly harder for her to push against the ED thoughts than it is for me) or choose to have a no self-bullying zone in my head.

I no longer wanted to put myself under pressure to be perfect. It was time to change that underwear, let the slinging commence and throw that belief out once and for all. I checked my definition of being a perfect mum, as the old one wasn't serving me anymore. I spent time getting to know myself. I worked on identifying my core values and personal beliefs and began to realise that kindness, compassion, family, and understanding are a few of mine. I reminded myself that I needed to apply them to myself, not just others, and show self-compassion and kindness to myself.

So, when I was faced with the feeling that I was being judged, or not good enough, I reminded myself that, no matter who you come across, some people will like you and some will hate you. You can't control what people think about you but you can control how you think about it. It is not possible to please everyone, and that's OK.

Being comfortable with who I am is a big step change for me. I am learning to accept my flaws. I am impatient, easily frustrated at times, a people-pleaser, striving for perfection and am often hard on myself. I am big-hearted, compassionate and caring, with a desire to help and support others. I am no model, as happier in jeans and a hoodie, and rarely seen with makeup unless going out for a special occasion. I like that I can just be me but I can dress up when I choose to.

Being a parent is not about being a perfect parent, it is about being a good-enough parent. There will be days when we will lose our temper, when we are too tired to distract our loved ones from their ED thoughts, when we wish they would stop shouting and just eat, and when we don't want to get out of bed and face the day ahead. All of these are OK. It doesn't mean that we don't love our children, that we don't care, and that we are not perfect parents. It means that we are human, just like everyone else and that is OK.

Seeing the perfectionism trait in my daughter made me think that she learned it from me. When things hadn't gone quite the way she wanted, she would get upset and frustrated. Like the time when we sat on the sand, watching the tide come in, and we hadn't realised how wet the sand was or how not-waterproof the towel was that we were sitting on. Luckily her T-shirt covered her wet patch, but mine was obvious for everyone to see, a huge patch across the whole of my bottom. I walked around the pier with a very soggy pair of trousers that day. It was embarrassing but it lightened the mood as we both giggled at the sight. Her initial reaction was disappointment that the day hadn't worked out how she had wanted. I was able to tell her that if it had gone exactly how she wanted, yes, it would have been lovely, but we would have missed out on the giggles and the fun memory of our time together, which was more perfect to me than if it was perfect.

I may not be the perfect person I once craved to be, but I can see now that I no longer need to be, and I need to let this go so my children, especially Poppy, can also see it.

It won't happen overnight but, for me, letting go of perfectionism is being good enough.

44

I hate seeing the pain she is in

11th February 2022

Dear Diary,

I hate seeing the pain she is in.

I hate not being able to make it better for her.

I hate my life right now.

All my energy has been zapped out of me. Neither my body nor my brain wants to work and I can't move from this spot.

Nothing I am doing is helping. Every mealtime is so painful, the battles are relentless and she is leaving food again. How can things deteriorate so quickly? I can't go through all this again.

She says she wants to die. For a split second, I contemplated it too. Maybe I also want to be free of this pain. I feel weak and helpless. I am hurting with her and for her and I don't know if I can go through another 19 months of this.

I have lost my happy, fun-loving daughter. The person in front of me is a shell of who she was. She is exhausted, lost, broken and unmotivated. It is breaking my heart to see her like this, I wish I could swap places with her, I would do it in the blink of an eye. But I can't.

Her birthday wasn't far away and she still didn't want to celebrate. I was still torn not knowing what to do for the best. We always celebrate birthdays. Why should that year be any different?

I wanted to make it a fun time.

I wanted to show her that her life was worth living.

I wanted to make it better than the last year when we were only allowed one hour together due to the strict visiting times on the specialist unit.

On the other hand, I still didn't know whether to bother. Would she still be here or would she be spending her 16th birthday in the hospital?

I felt again like I was fighting another battle I couldn't win. I felt that I was fighting on my own and losing, whilst the ED was gaining more territory with each mealtime. Whatever strength she had was gone and there was no sign of it returning.

I expressed my concerns to CAMHS so many times, as well as the need to address her weight, but it was dismissed time for time and they told me it was more about her state than her weight. I understood the need to look at the wider picture, not to focus on weight, and for Poppy to see there was more to life than the ED, but her weight and mood continued to plummet. She was nearly the same weight as in July 2020 when she was first admitted and the only difference was that her blood pressure and pulse remained normal. I was scared that it is only a matter of time till they plummeted too.

Everything I wanted to say came tumbling out as I poured my heart out to CAMHS, with all the pent-up frustration and emotions I had kept under wraps. They were also really concerned. I wanted to say, "Better late than never." They were considering stopping school, and a hospital admission looked likely.

I finally felt listened to and it was reassuring that we were on the same page at last. They discussed that a hospital or a specialist unit might not be the best place for her as it was likely to send her into a downward spiral, as Poppy was a home-bird. But no alternative solution was given, so I was no clearer about what could be done.

The walking was stopped, to conserve energy, which didn't go down well with Poppy. She seemed to lose all hope, and her eating deteriorated further, and no meal was properly finished.

Her ED thoughts returned with full force and gave her ammunition to eat less because the walking was stopped. She couldn't accept that she still needed to eat everything.

It was as if she had given up, and the intensity of the guilt and shame had multiplied. More reminders had to be given to clear her plate, but were met with more groans, grumbles, and shouting, "I can't do it." Common statements at mealtimes were, "I feel sick" or "I feel full" and it was as if we were looking back to where we had been many months previously.

She felt that life had been ripped away from her, yet again, and she couldn't see any point in trying and thus no point in living. Everything that was once enjoyable had ceased and she felt that she was being punished. It was not true but that was how she felt.

Unfortunately, having Covid a few weeks ago didn't help and, with the extra stress she was under with her exams, it was difficult to halt the weight loss. In such a short space of time, it had made a big impact on her life and her mood. No wonder she felt devastated and punished, as she was grieving the life that she had worked hard to get.

She had been doing so well, getting her freedom back, and developing an identity outside the ED. It was uplifting to see, and I thought we were climbing and taking time to enjoy the scenery. Then BOOM. It came from nowhere and her life was blown up into smithereens.

I hoped that she could turn it around, but I wasn't sure if she could. I didn't want her to go back to the hospital, but something needed to be done. I was going to try to turn it around in two weeks before going back to the MDT (Multidisciplinary Team) to review her progress.

My mind was in a spin, churning all my worries and fears, another night of tossing and turning as I waited for the time to get up and face the day ahead.

Poppy was barely hanging on. She had no desire to keep living, but couldn't see a way out. She went between not wanting to live and having to live for me and her brother. The mental exhaustion, the pressure from the exams, and the pressure to stop eating were too much for her.

She couldn't see what an amazing person she was. I saw a girl who was loving, kind, gentle, caring, compassionate, friendly, creative, amazing, clever, courageous, strong, a survivor, resilient, a warrior and beautiful, both inside and out, patient, thoughtful and so much more. I saw someone who was much more than what she saw in the reflection or the number on the scales.

I was on the countdown, waiting for the MDT appointment, whilst watching her get thinner and weaker. I couldn't help but stare as her lovely face and inner glow vanished in front of my eyes. Replaced by a face so gaunt and tired, with her sunken cheeks and prominent teeth, her body resembled a middle-aged woman rather than a teenager. Memories flooded back of when she last looked like that. She seemed to be eating better but her body showed no signs of improvement. My heart was breaking as her body was showing signs that the ED had again taken hold, and I was not sure what damage it was doing inside.

I was stunned when she came downstairs and then went straight back to bed. She must have been exhausted as she wouldn't normally allow herself to do that, as the thoughts in her head would be cruel. I hoped that being in bed wouldn't stop her from eating, as her head would probably reason that she didn't need as much food.

I was prepared to take her to A&E, if necessary. There were signs that her body was struggling to cope; the exhaustion, feeling cold and she was cold to the touch.

We had planned to go to Wales for a few days over half-term, but we decided that she wasn't well enough to go. She wouldn't be able to sit in the car for that length of time and wasn't well enough to walk any distance. CAMHS were hesitant about us going and asked me if I knew where the nearest hospital was, just in case. Hearing that, blew my mind. We were not going.

Wales was a special place for us both so rescheduling was the best thing to do, since the great memories over the years needed to be kept as that and not replaced by the challenges and hardships that she currently faced.

What was going to happen? How was she going to get better? How long would it take to get back to where she was? How much pain was she going to have to go through? Where would she end up? Could she survive another time in the hospital?

I didn't have the answers and there was no quick fix. She was exhausted by the thoughts, she went to bed and hoped every morning that the voices would have gone, but they were still there, as cruel and bullying as ever.

How does one cope with listening to that every day? I can't imagine. I struggle when I have a headache and can't think properly and sleeping sometimes is the only thing that helps me, but I know that the pain will have gone in the morning. But for her, it remains, and maybe even intensifies.

45

Life is like a jigsaw

Poppy loves jigsaws. They became part of her daily life in the hospital where she would spend hours doing them. I don't have the patience to find all the pieces, whereas Poppy finds it relaxing.

She finds it helpful when I relate her ED journey to a jigsaw puzzle. Just like the puzzle, there are times when things run smoothly and slot into place, and times when it is challenging and you can't find any pieces that fit. No matter how hard or how long you try, it seems unattainable.

I spent so much time trying to find solutions and missing pieces; anything that could reach her so that she would start to fight against the ED.

When she struggled to eat, I explained that it was like putting a piece of the jigsaw in, back to front and upside down. Each time she engaged in compensatory behaviours, another piece would be put in wrongly. The picture would no longer be clear or resemble the life she deserved to have. In my eyes, she deserves a happy, extraordinary life but, unfortunately, we are not on the same page, as she doesn't see that yet.

Our lives can feel relentless at times, and we can lose sight of where we are going and what we want to achieve. Seeing all the pieces that need putting together can be overwhelming. It can be tempting to discard the puzzle as it's too difficult and frustrating, it's easier to give up.

That was me. Others could identify pieces that I couldn't see. They saw things slipping, such as when she crept back into the kitchen. I saw that as being like the old days, but they saw it for what it was, her trying to influence what was being prepared.

Poppy and I had different ideas for the jigsaw picture. She wanted the ED in her life, always in the background, whereas I wanted to rip it out, for her to create her own jigsaw which was free of rules, demands and harsh bullying.

I worked hard to help her find each piece, only to realise that the ED had either discarded some or replaced them with upside-down pieces where you couldn't see the picture.

It is soul-destroying when you're so close to making out part of the picture and then realise that important pieces are missing and the picture has been ruined and cannot be completed.

Perhaps this has happened to you. You may have felt like giving up, your patience may have faded and you might not have been able to put a single piece in for days. You feel you have no option but to quit and discard the puzzle as it's too hard and you don't want to do it anymore.

But you have no choice. Your loved one needs you and you must start all over again. The picture that you once hoped for has changed and you can no longer complete it as those pieces are missing. You must refocus on piecing together a more achievable puzzle, a new one that fits better. This may be upsetting as you have worked hard and come so far, and now you have to start again.

Many of us go through life feeling something is missing, or we try to find a way to make the pieces fit. The difficult times can help us find those pieces and we can use them to shape our lives.

It is important not to lose sight of the picture that you are trying to work on. It may not be achievable right now, but each small jigsaw piece you add is another step closer to where you want to be. I gained hope with each piece we added, believing that we would get there.

Just like a jigsaw puzzle with many pieces, it takes time, resilience and patience. There might be moments when you will want to give up, but if you want to complete the picture, you need to keep finding the right pieces so that you can achieve what you set out to. Supporting someone with ED is similar. You will want to give up, want someone else to complete it, want to hide from it, but the longer you do this, the longer it will take you to accomplish it.

Don't forget that there are moments in life when everything clicks, the pieces slot together and the picture is nearly complete. When that happens, everything feels right in the world.

Our jigsaw was looking rosy and I felt happier. More pieces were coming together and the picture was looking great. Then, unfortunately, some pieces started to fall out. I hadn't taken my eye off it but we had to start a new one. It was smaller but still hard to complete. It involved us getting through the following few weeks with Poppy's Mock Exams. Then we will focus on another small jigsaw, taking each piece at a time.

We learn from a young age that, if we want something, we have to go and get it. I would chat with Poppy and explain that if she wants a different life, she can choose what she wants to achieve, and she is the one that can put the pieces together to make it a reality.

Our loved ones hold all the pieces to overcome the ED, but they don't always use them or want to use them. Depending on what stage they are at on their journey, we might need to put those pieces in the puzzle for them, guide them to the next piece or watch from a distance, ready to take over if they remove the pieces and put their picture at risk.

Each time they go against the ED's thoughts and rules, another piece is added and it is another win.

I wish that Poppy could see that recovery is worth it as much as I can. I wish all the sufferers battling an eating disorder, or another illness, could see this but they are sometimes too poorly to see what they are doing and the impact it is having.

The struggle to find the pieces will test them, but we can be there to remind them to keep going, to keep looking and place a new piece. Rather than quitting, it is better to break the puzzle down into manageable bits, so they can be reminded of how far they have come and how much they have achieved.

Each piece and each small jigsaw that Poppy completes will ultimately take us closer to the wider picture of her having the life she deserves. I am hoping that she will see this and, in time, she will see that it was worth it. I look forward to standing and admiring the view when she has completed it. It will be the best jigsaw puzzle that we have ever done together.

"Imagine all of our lives are like our own individual jigsaw puzzles. As we're going through life, we're just slowly piecing it together, bit by bit, based on experiences and lessons that we've learned, until we get the best picture." Daniel Sloss

"Life is like a jigsaw puzzle, you have to see the whole picture, then put it together piece by piece." Terry McMillan.

46

Is grass green or blue?

The extreme power and control that the ED had on my daughter's thoughts were unbelievable. I assumed that it would somehow fade, but it didn't.

It was hard to understand until I thought about it differently. For example, the colour of grass. Go with me, dear friend. The ED would tell Poppy that grass was blue and no amount of persuasion could convince her that it was green; everyone else was wrong.

There were times when she would see the colour green, but doubt would creep in and the ED was so convincing that she could no longer see it as it was, despite questioning whether she should listen to her head or everyone else. Some days she would fight against the thoughts and green would win, but on others when the ED was too powerful, the grass remained blue. I wish it was as simple as the colour of grass, but the ED impacted so much of her life; what she believed and felt about herself, what she thought she saw, and much more. It was scary to see the power that it had over her.

16th February 2022 was a particularly difficult day. Her Mock Exams brought daily struggles and distress, her anxiety increased around mealtimes, and the pain from the ED thoughts worsened.

We were trying to hold on, as there were only two more days of exams. I suspected that she was crumbling inside and I hoped that the pressure would soon lift. I didn't understand why she put so much pressure on herself to do well. It didn't help to reassure her that they are just practice tests, so that she and the teachers could see the areas she needed to work on and that her health was more important than exams. Every mealtime was a challenge, with her saying, "I can't eat, I don't want to eat, I feel sick and have no appetite."

The noise in her head was incredible. Who wouldn't want to stop it? We all would, especially when faced with an important exam or presentation where you need your full concentration. Not eating in times of difficulty was her default, but it had to change as it was a slippery slope and there was only one way that it would head if she didn't eat enough.

I hugged her and told her that I couldn't ever know what she was going through, but I could imagine that she might be feeling exhausted, anxious, not wanting to eat, and wanting the pain to end. I told her that I loved her. I chatted to her about how I had felt when I took my exams, allowing her to open up and talk about her feelings.

I used to get stressed with exams but not to the extent that she did. She constantly felt in a state of anxiety and tried to find a way to cope by restricting food and revising every hour she could. She desperately wanted to restrict but my daily mantra was repeated regularly, "Eating is non-negotiable, you have to eat."

The stress was making the ED's voice louder. Hearing that she didn't feel that she deserved to eat was hard to stomach, no one should ever feel that they must earn food, regardless of whether they haven't done enough revision or haven't walked enough.

It helped to validate how Poppy was feeling, even if I didn't understand or agree with her viewpoint, as it calmed her and made her feel less alone. I hugged her when I heard how hard it was for her, hearing what the ED was saying. No wonder she was in pieces. No wonder she felt as if she was breaking, having to listen to it every single day. Every. Single. Day. With no rest.

Breakfast times were getting worse. It was clear she was not in a great place. She would stare at the food, her shoulders down and her face showing a level of anxiety. Time was ticking for her to go to school and no amount of encouragement got her to eat. I talked to her again about reducing her revision time, having breaks, reducing the number of exams, considering putting the exams on hold and concentrating on her recovery, as her health was more important. But she always refused.

I didn't think she was well enough to do her exams, but I couldn't get her to see that. She was doing an excessive amount of revision, with few or no breaks, no fun, and no self-care. She was heading towards exhaustion and burnout.

I reiterated how much I loved her, and how hard it must be for her, but it was important to eat her breakfast and, if she wasn't able to eat, then, unfortunately, I couldn't take her to school. Her body needed food. It was non-negotiable. I thought I would get some push-back but there was none, and she eventually ate. Phew! It was painful to watch, as each mouthful was slow and mechanical. She needed prompts to finish her cereal, juice and fruit and encouragement to keep sitting.

She went to school but, inside, she was barely holding on. She didn't want to live and her pain was intense. Maybe I should have pulled her from the exams but she was adamant that she was doing them and there was nothing I could do to stop her. But at what cost?

It felt as if I was waiting for something to happen. I didn't know what, but I could feel something was coming. She was like a pressure cooker, with the pressure building, and I was struggling to reduce the heat. When it did go off, I wasn't sure how messy it would be. Would she stop eating completely? Would she self-harm, or worse? I didn't know. All I could do was wait and watch. I regularly told CAMHS how worried I was but they did nothing.

I held back the tears. I wasn't sure how much more I could take, seeing her drive herself into the ground. The revision was non-stop, no matter what I said or did.

My bomb defences were back on, although at times they slipped, leaving me exposed and vulnerable to the stresses and strains. Hearing her words tumble out, "I can't do it, it's too hard," were sometimes too painful. I reminded myself to hold on. When she finished her Mock Exams, I was waiting for the fallout. It came.

She spiralled out of control and her weight decreased again. Her body and mind were weak because of the previous few weeks.

She had nothing left to cope. She lifted her sleeve and her arm was covered in blood. I could make out seven or eight cuts on her arm. I went into rescue mode and started cleaning and dressing them, not realising that the first-aid Poppy needed was for me to hug her. The dressings could wait.

Maybe I did judge, although I didn't mean to. I recognised that it was Poppy's way of coping, but I just wish that she didn't have to cut herself.

We all have different ways of coping, and there is no right or wrong. It's about how we can manage our world, our pain, and our struggles.

I still find it hard seeing the scars, as they symbolise how much she was struggling.

I always wanted the same things: for her not to struggle anymore and to live a life without the ED.

With each new scar, I saw the turmoil that she was still in, and it hurt me.

I knew that she was fighting her ED thoughts each day, but I hadn't realised that she was also fighting the need to self-harm.

She described it as losing control and being unable to think clearly, and all she could focus on was a need to cut herself. Her pain continued to build and that was the only way to vent it.

Some of her scars have faded, some are much more prominent, and others have taken time to heal. Just like the scars heal with time, she will too. I see the scars as a reflection of her struggle, but hopefully, one day I will see them as a reminder of her strength and resilience against the battles she overcame.

47

The annoying backseat driver

Although it was days until her birthday, I couldn't shake the feeling that she wouldn't be at home then. I wanted to celebrate, just in case, but I wasn't sure how to as she was so tired and weak.

It was a good opportunity to try out my new thinking and reset our focus away from the ED. Maybe it would help her too. There I go again, switching into 'fix it' mode.

I got some great ideas by reaching out to friends on Facebook and surprised Poppy by having some early birthday fun. Changing her hair colour was a good one; she loved that, and although sitting in the salon was extremely hard, she did it. The online art lesson was also great, followed by watching a show at the theatre. I would like to say that the day was perfect, but that would be a lie. The elephant in the room was still there as her eating was still not great. I tried to get her to eat everything, which caused animosity, but the overall day was good and gave us a few moments without the ED.

Having all of us at home during half-term was lovely and we did normal stuff. All her friends were talking about the prom and she wanted to go, so dress shopping was the next thing planned that week. It was still five months away, which gave her time to get stronger and be in a better place.

The Mock Exams had a huge impact on Poppy. Trying hard not to have a defeatist attitude, I wasn't sure if she would be well enough to take the GCSEs a few months later. Maybe we were putting a sticky plaster on, for her to rip it off again when she took the main exams. She hadn't recovered from the Mock Exams and was still exhausted. I never thought I would hear her say that she was glad that she wasn't going for a walk, as she was too tired. I hoped that the week out of school would help her to rest, but I didn't hold out much as the ED was too strong.

The MDT was the following day and her anxiety was building. She admitted that part of her wanted to go into the hospital and the other part knew that it would push her further towards hell. She saw that she had two options. Staying in the current hell loop or going through it to get to the other side. Either would be awful.

I thought a hospital admission was going to be necessary; not to give me a rest, but to get her back on track. As awful as it would be as an outsider again, watching and waiting for her to come through it, I thought she needed that. We were in a holding bay, watching which way it would go. Would her stats deteriorate enough for her to be admitted? How would she eat? These would have an impact on which way it went.

I love my analogues. When chatting to my brother about Poppy's illness, we likened her to the driver of a car, where the destination was influenced by her ED thoughts. I was the passenger who sometimes slipped into being the annoying backseat driver, calling out instructions and offering unwanted advice, so that we would keep travelling in the direction I wanted to go, rather than where she wanted to go. Like any backseat driver, I preferred to be in control rather than be a passenger and found it difficult to watch the ED take control of the driving.

I struggled to stop myself from grabbing the steering wheel and driving the car myself. I constantly refrained from altering the Sat Nav, resisted the temptation to accelerate, and avoided the urge to keep driving without stopping at any roadblocks. I felt helpless and it was exhausting trying to seize control, and impossible to overcome the defeatism that took hold. I wanted to throw my hands in the air and give up.

I found myself pushing for a particular route, inputting an address without questioning or listening, grasping the wheel tightly, trying a different approach, and shifting into a different gear. Meanwhile, I tried to be empathetic and an open listener with a gentle coaching approach. However, no matter how kind-hearted my intentions were, I wasn't always the best passenger for the journey.

I felt frustrated and helpless. I constantly saw the same roads, with the familiar park benches, as we circled the same roundabouts, time and time again. With no end in sight, our destination was still far away.

We can often see the direction our loved ones need to take but if their focus doesn't shift, despite our encouragement and endless attempts to change their internal navigation, their original route will not alter and they will continue driving around with the same views.

When a car breaks down, help is needed. This may be a quick repair on the side of the road, or it may require towing to a garage for further repair and parts. When our loved one needs help, they may need support from us, healthcare services or a hospital stay to get them back on track and complete their onward journey.

There may be multiple times when the driver needs to go down the same roads, or the car needs to go back to the garage for repairs. That was us at that point. I desperately wanted to put my foot on the accelerator and get Poppy to our destination as quickly as we could. But she had other ideas and, with her foot hovering over the brake, she was slowly reversing in the opposite direction.

It is a difficult balance when your loved one's life is at stake. Do you yank the steering wheel with all your strength? Do you allow them to make their own mistakes? Do you accompany them on the journey and step in when necessary? It is extremely frustrating to be close to the destination and then realise that the car has done a 360-degree turn and you are back at the beginning again. The same roads ahead are to be navigated again. Knowing that they are coming up doesn't make it any easier. It's harder, as you remember each turn and each bump on the road.

I have had to come to terms with Poppy being the driver of her life. I am only the passenger, there to support her but I can't drive the car for her.

I have spent a lot of time grabbing the wheel, trying to keep Poppy on track. As well as being the passenger, I have also tried to be the garage and the mechanic, which hasn't always been helpful. When I grab the wheel, it is my default mode to fix everything; like I did when she was younger and grazed her knees from a fall. But I can see now that it is not always the right thing to do, as it affects how she learns to fix things for herself. I thought I was doing the right thing, but I have been grabbing the wheel too often and for too long; not necessarily just with this illness but maybe with other parts of her life. It saddens me that it has taken until now to see this, although it is better to be aware so that I can start making changes.

I need to work on balance to give Poppy her freedom so that she can learn to navigate through accidents, roadblocks, traffic jams and detours herself, yet be ready to steer or grab the wheel when she is in danger and needs help.

It may take longer for her to get there but she will reach her destination. I will still be the passenger, making sure that she has the right fuel. Encouraging her to take time to pause and embrace the scenery, be inspired by the people she meets, always believing that she will get there, and remind her that it may not turn out the way she first anticipated, but that's OK. She may prefer a different destination, one that fits better.

However, I am not going to lose myself on this journey and let it consume my daily life. I will ride with her, as I offer guidance and support, but I will show her that there are better roads for us to travel on and better destinations to be explored together, away from the ED.

Belief is important. The last time she was admitted to the hospital, she navigated the twists and turns. Surely, she can do the same again. This time, I hope that she will get further before hitting a roadblock and keep pushing forward to find her way to her destination, no matter how long it takes.

48

No, not again!

The day of the MDT came and, as I saw it, there were two options: admission to the hospital or an ultimatum for her to turn it around, otherwise, she would be admitted. Either would be hard and I didn't want her to hurt anymore.

She didn't need to say anything and I could tell she was worried about the appointment. I was too, but for different reasons. She was scared that she would be admitted, which meant she would have to eat and her greatest fear would come true, that she would become fat. I was scared that, if they didn't do anything, I would have to watch her get weaker before they eventually stepped in. Something had to be done as we couldn't carry on as we were. She was going backwards and I couldn't stop it.

Poppy went in, while I waited in the reception and tried to read my book to take my mind off things. I couldn't concentrate as too many thoughts were whizzing around my head. Surely, they had to do something.

I was right. I had hoped that her weight might have stabilised but she had lost a significant amount and her heart showed more signs of being affected.

No, not again!

They wanted to admit her. A mixture of emotions flooded through me: relief, that they were finally listening and going to do something, and despair that I was right, and that she was as poorly as I had thought.

She refused, and no amount of persuasion could get her to agree to be admitted. They arranged to see her again the following week.

That night, she ate very little and it was as if she had given up. To her, if she was going in, then what was the point of eating? It was far better to give up. I wanted to scream at her, "No. Regardless of whether you go in or not, you still must eat."

She was so poorly. She was not capable of seeing the big picture. The further she fell, the further she had to come back. She admitted to restricting, something I thought she was doing but wasn't able to catch her in the act. She needed help.

She was in denial. I hoped that when she had time to process it, she would agree to the admission. Despite her not wanting to go, I pushed them for a bed, but there were none available and we were advised to wait until the following Monday. Meanwhile, I persuaded her to keep eating and wouldn't allow her to do any activity. She hated it and pushed back constantly. It wasn't easy.

It was a difficult balance to get right, but by trying to get her to accept that she needed to go to the hospital, she gave up and had a 'what's the point?' mentality. She still had the mindset, 'If I'm going in, then why bother eating? Why not surrender to it?' Her mood, her eating and all the compensatory behaviours got worse. There were still no beds available. It was a dangerous tactic for her to play.

I changed tack and encouraged her to see that she was in control and knew what to do. She began to eat more. It wasn't easy and required a lot of persuasion and encouragement, and her standing remained a problem, but at least she was eating.

It made me cringe to see the prominence of her spine and shoulder blades. When she got that thin, it was hard to bounce back. Not just her appearance, but the impact it had on her, as her world imploded. She was no longer able to do anything, yet she still couldn't see the impact that the ED had.

Out of desperation, I pointed out to her that her spine was protruding, a sure sign that she was too thin, but it was what she wanted. She recognised that she was cold and tired, however, there was a part of her that liked feeling that way. She didn't believe that she was poorly enough to go into hospital.

It scared me when her lips went slightly blue. She told me that she felt cold and, despite the heating being on, she took to wearing her coat inside. Her hands had been cold for some time but now her feet were also cold, despite wearing fleecy boots. Things were deteriorating and CAMHS advised me to contact the doctor.

The GP confirmed that her blood pressure was low and contacted the paediatrics for advice. Waiting to hear was nerve-racking. Everything was up in the air. Her 16th birthday was only three days away but it was difficult to plan for it, as she was not well enough. The prom dress fitting shopping appointment was booked for two days away but it was unlikely that she was going to be able to go. I was glad that I had arranged an early celebration for her.

One of my awful habits is overthinking and questions would pop into my head and whizz around. How long will this hospital stay be? Would she exercise in the bathroom again? Would she push against everything they said and did? Would she go backwards before going forwards? Would she need a bed in a Specialist Eating Unit? Will she get better this time?

No wonder my head ached and the familiar unwell feeling lay heavily again. It was time to use the advice I had given Poppy, "Tell yourself to stop. Visualise a stop sign in front of you. Repeat and say it louder: Stop, Stop, STOP! Breathe in, breathe out, and be in the here and now."

To be back at the start of our journey was soul-destroying, especially as we knew what was ahead of us, yet again. Frustration, anger and sadness didn't sufficiently describe how I was feeling. I had seen her get weaker and thinner, whilst the ED thoughts got stronger. I had asked CAMHS to help and had put my faith in them.

Poppy's eating had improved, although it was too little too late. She said to me, "I have a bit more energy, I think it is because I am eating more." I wanted to say, "Who knew that eating would give you more energy and that you would feel better?!" But I didn't as it wouldn't have helped.

The GP rang to confirm that the hospital would ring later. The morning went by so slowly and I was willing the phone to ring, checking to see if there had been any missed calls. I couldn't settle to do anything, worried that they would refuse to take her in.

CAMHS rang and a bed was available.

Even though it was what she needed, it hit me that I had also been in denial. Part of me had clung on to the hope that she wasn't that bad and the other part wanted the admission so that she could get help. I had been burying my head in the sand hoping that it would all go away, hoping that everything would be OK. Deep down, I knew that it wasn't. The phone call sent me into a panic. How was I going to tell her? Would she go? How was I going to persuade her to go? I wept for a while, absorbing the news. I didn't want this to happen, but it needed to.

As soon as I saw Poppy and her brother, I hugged them both and the tears flowed. They knew. I didn't even have to say the words, they could tell. I kept saying sorry, that this was so hard for her and I knew she didn't want to go in, but we had no choice as she was too unwell and needed to so that she could get better. I told her that I was going to miss her. I told her that she could do it, and I told her she could beat it. I needed to hear that as much as she did.

We clung to each other, absorbing the realisation that we would be separated again for a while. Uncertainty surrounded us.

I went into automatic pilot, collecting and packing clothes, toiletries, headphones, books, chargers; anything that I thought she would need. The hospital wanted us there in less than two hours, so she spent precious time snuggling and playing with the dog and saying goodbyes. The time we had together went so quickly. I tried to keep my emotions in check so as not to make it harder for her but I was aware of the lump in my throat. Getting her into the car wasn't easy as she didn't want to go. I didn't want her to either but there was no choice.

Feelings of guilt hit me. I had been pushing for this to happen yet when faced with it, I questioned if it was the right thing to do. Could I have tried harder? We both cried on the journey. This would be her third admission, and it brought back many memories.

Walking onto the ward must have been hard for her, not knowing how long it would be until she would return home. I wondered if she experienced a little comfort from seeing familiar faces. I suspected that the memories of the difficulties she overcame and the familiarity of being placed in the same bed, next to the nurses' station, would hit her, maybe not straight away, but at some point.

Leaving her was hard. It never got any easier. I felt like the bad guy again, pushing for the admission. I had to remember that there was no other option, and if she had stayed at home she would have died. That was not an option.

I couldn't make sense of my emotions. I felt overwhelmed with guilt for being a failure and letting her down again, yet I felt relieved that something was happening at last.

Walking into the house, it was empty of her presence again. I didn't know what to do. My tummy was in knots and my eyes were sore and blotchy from crying. I felt lost. I couldn't face being in the house on my own, so I took the dog for a walk. I needed to process what had happened and how I was feeling.

It helped clear my head, as I realised that I couldn't change what had happened, so there was no point dwelling on it.

I wanted to reach out to Poppy, to make sure that she was OK, but decided against it as she also needed processing time.

It was lovely to hear her voice later, but not so to hear her distress as she hated being there. It pulled at my heartstrings and I repeated that she was in the right place. I wasn't sure who needed to hear that more, her or me; I suspect both. I wished her goodnight and told her that I would see her the next day. She sobbed down the phone and begged me to take her home.

What was ahead weighed on me and I was not looking forward to seeing her in the hospital; her distress at having to eat and wanting to escape from the agonising mental and physical pain.

Getting to sleep was easy as I was exhausted, but staying asleep was a different matter as there was too much whirling in my head. I couldn't believe that we were back there again, with her third admission in 19 months. Getting up at 5 am to work became the norm as it was better to do something productive than lie in bed, tossing and turning and getting more frustrated that I wasn't able to sleep.

Poppy felt that she didn't have any energy to make it through. I didn't know if I did either.

They tell you to rest, but they don't tell you how to do that. I'm not sure how possible it is when your daughter is so unwell. Her self-harming had restarted, the suicidal thoughts had returned, and she daily begged to come home and pleaded endlessly, "I can do this at home, Mum!"

I wanted to believe her but, only two days ago, she had been hiding food in the bin, so why did she want to get better now and think that she could? She said she would eat anything, work on her sitting when told and stay out of the kitchen. I so wanted to believe her but they often want to come home so that they can restrict again; like a vicious circle.

I made a commitment that, whilst she was in the hospital, my life would go on. I enjoyed my new sense of freedom, although it was tarnished by knowing how much she was struggling in the hospital. I tried to put that to the back of my mind. It was refreshing to be able to go to the shops, meet friends, grab a coffee, and have a meal without having to watch the time or negotiate with her to eat. I needed to put myself first, charge my batteries, and have some time away from the ED world so that I would be prepared for when she came home.

I was torn between balancing work commitments, spending time with Jordan and my mum, visiting Poppy and some 'me' time. One of the first things I did was ring Jordan on the way home from the hospital to ask if he wanted to go out for dinner, something we were normally unable to do. It was refreshing to chat over a meal with no anxiety. My time with him was special and I felt that I was reconnecting with myself; something I had neglected to do for a long time.

My good intentions didn't last. The messages I received from Poppy knocked me for six and I felt pulled in multiple directions, leaving me little, or no time, for myself.

Seeing some progress of Poppy sitting down in the ward was a great boost, something she hadn't been able to do for some time. It was twinged with a little sadness, as I found myself slipping into thoughts of, "Was I not assertive enough, not strong enough and not capable enough to get her to sit at home?" The spiky monster was in good form. Were those questions helpful? No, they weren't, so I let them pass by me, like a box on a conveyor belt, so that I could focus on what I was doing.

I am not sure what I would have done if my employer hadn't been so supportive and accommodating to allow me to work flexibly. I was able to juggle work, visiting times, spending time with my son, running the house, and supporting my mum whose health had deteriorated rapidly. It was a scary and worrying time. It didn't help that I had used all my sick leave entitlement and had no backup plan. I thought that she had been doing so well and that we had finally cracked it. I was wrong … or naïve.

I craved to be just a mum, but even though I made a point of not getting involved with what she was or wasn't eating on the ward, I found it impossible not to step into the role of coach, cheerleader and therapist. How can you not when your child is suffering? She desperately wanted the pain to stop and there were many times when she wanted to take her last breath. Hearing your child want to end their life is beyond earth-shattering. I am not sure if I will ever get over that.

The hospital rang late one night. She had only been there for one day and she had cut her arm in about ten places. She had used a sharpener which she had taken with her from home. I didn't even know that we had sharpeners at home. I had packed for her but hadn't realised that she had snuck it in when I wasn't looking.

I was so cross with myself.

49

F for failure

A week later, despite the staff checking her belongings, she hurt herself again. She was then put on a one-to-one. She hated having someone there all the time, even through the night, but it was necessary to keep her safe. Her mental health had been bad in the past, but it was at a new level.

I was met with little compassion when I reached out to CAMHS and shared that Poppy continued to beg me to move on with my life and forget her. They said that it was going to take time to get the right nutrition so that she could start to improve. If only it had been that easy. It should have been. When you leave your loved ones in someone else's care there is an unwritten trust that they will be kept safe. I hadn't expected the hospital to break that trust.

I couldn't understand why she wasn't gaining weight. I had expected her to lose weight the first week just as she had done previously but it continued week after week. Her skin became paler, her bones more prominent, her face gaunter, and even more worryingly, her heart rate continued to decrease into the low 30s.

I couldn't shake the nagging doubt of knowing where this was heading. I had tried my very best to stop her from deteriorating. I had tried to get help. I had tried to get them to listen. I couldn't squash the resentment building up inside of me. I had been asking for help so many times, but each time I failed to get anywhere.

Looking back, of course, there were things that I could have done differently but I was doing my best at the time.

The CAMHS nurse arranged to see me and began asking about Poppy's meal plan at home. It was like being transported back in front of the headteacher, explaining why you hadn't finished your homework on time. Each silence was painful, each comment felt like a red pen marking my homework. She made it clear that Poppy's eating was my fault. The homework was marked, and the grade was a big red F for failure.

I told her that I had repeatedly asked for help. I told them that the meal plan wasn't right and that she needed help. I told them that I couldn't get her to eat anything else. Somehow it felt as if it was all my fault, the responsibility and failure were now firmly at my door, not theirs. I wasn't looking to blame anyone; I just didn't want to be in that situation again. It was hard to shrug off the big red F grade that I felt I had been given. It weighed heavily on me and, no matter how many times I kept saying that I was doing my best, the weight remained.

I started to overanalyse the previous months, weeks and days, looking for what I had done wrong. It was important to Poppy to take her Mock Exams, but she was too intensely focused on them, and no amount of reasoning would change her mind. I didn't know how huge the impact was at the time, although some things were easy to spot; the increased meal distress, holding food in her mouth ready to spit it out, the standing, and the daily panic attacks. But I didn't see the whole picture. I hadn't seen her exercising, hiding the food or the severe restriction, especially towards the end. I didn't know how I had missed that, but I needed to take my own advice. I can either beat myself up or learn from it and make changes to prevent it from happening again.

It appeared that when she ate at my mum's, there was little distress. I questioned her as to why being there helped. The alarm bells didn't dampen down in my head, as something wasn't right, and I didn't trust her. My gut instinct was correct as I discovered that she managed to tip some of her food into the bin. I had been outsmarted again. The pieces slotted together. She would say to my mum that her food was cold and, when she was warming it up, used the opportunity to dispose of some of it. No wonder she found it easier to eat there. My mum's health was not great at the time and, with hindsight, it wasn't the best idea to allow her to go there but it gave me a much-needed break.

I kicked myself over that for a while, but it wasn't just at my mum's. She took any opportunity that was there.

50

Sweet sixteen

It was Poppy's birthday, and she was now sixteen. Sweet sixteen, although there was nothing sweet about her life at that moment.

It seemed to be a birthday tradition for her to spend her celebrations either in a hospital or a specialist unit.

The ward staff were amazing, as they did their best to make the day as special as they could, decorating the ward and her bed with balloons and banners.

I tried to make it as special as I could. The staff passed on a box which contained envelopes, each with a written note, a photo and a letter. Poppy had to spell the letters out to reveal 'Happy Birthday'. I bought a birthday cake, not for eating, as that would have sent her into complete panic, but for all of us to sing 'Happy Birthday' to her. It was something we did every year and I didn't want her to miss out because of the ED.

Despite being the only one allowed to visit Poppy, due to the Covid restrictions, she had a nice birthday, and we planned to celebrate again in style when she was better.

Let's hope there will be no hospital in sight for her 17th birthday.

51

Mum, I want to die

No sooner had we enjoyed happy moments, than we found ourselves quickly coming back down with a bump. Though no one could ever predict the size of the bump.

Mum, I want to die. Please let me die.

I can't do this anymore. The pain is unbearable.

I want you to get on with your own life and let me die.

What do you say when your child says this to you?

I couldn't say anything for a while. I hugged her so hard and tried not to cry. The familiar lump in my throat and butterflies in my tummy were there again.

I empathised with her that things sounded awful, which was understandable, and I loved her so very much. Although she might not see it right now, her life will get better. She has to hold on. I am there for her, we all are. She can get through this and she will. Life will be different. This is not forever, just for now, and how she is feeling will pass. She needs to hold on to her hopes and dreams and focus on them.

In my wildest dreams, or should that be nightmares, I would never have envisaged my daughter's life to be like this. I expected normal things like falling out with friends, me moaning at the state of her bedroom, not tidying up after herself, failing a test and having a broken heart. I expected to hit some challenges through her teenage years, but I never expected to come close to her dying or wanting to die.

Life doesn't always work out the way you want. Curveballs happen which change our direction. They aren't planned or wanted and can send us off-course. However, how we adapt to these changes is up to us.

My daughter, having an eating disorder, was the most incredible curveball that we had experienced. I didn't see it coming and was not able to prepare for it. I certainly didn't know how to adapt and preferred to be in denial, at least at first.

I always thought that, out of my children, it would be my son that would be more affected after losing his dad. He was and remains to be, a closed book, as he doesn't talk about his feelings or losses; whereas Poppy would regularly have opened up and talked to me. I assumed that she was doing OK. How wrong I was.

Eating disorder curveballs need to be grabbed quickly before the course of direction is too difficult to turn around. They can come at you from different directions, at different times, and can change rapidly. There were many times when I was caught out and didn't notice until it was too late, and then it was much harder to get back from where we found ourselves.

We had experienced plenty of curveballs. Battling to cease the weight loss, trying to address the standing and running around, the headbutting, the self-harm, hiding and spitting out food, and the suicidal ideation. They were just the curveballs relating to Poppy. I also had worries about job security, finances and my mum's health.

As bad as things got, I always had a choice. Give up or get up.

There was no way I was giving up and I was not prepared to let Poppy give up either.

She mentioned that there was a tiny part of her that didn't want to die, so I asked her to listen to that part, no matter how quiet it was. That part needed her to listen, hold on and not give up.

52

Hope was all I had

Poppy messaged that she was scared that she could die, as she had been told that her heart was so weak it could give up. Despite the panic hitting her like a ton of bricks, she still couldn't bring herself to eat enough or drink the Fortisip. She was so ill that dying was an easier option than eating.

I asked for reassurance. I suppose I was grasping for the hope that everything was in hand and there was a plan to stop her deterioration. I told them that I didn't want to lose her. Their response was always the same. "Let's keep with the plan."

If the plan was to allow her to continue deteriorating, then it was working. I worried more as each day passed.

8th March 2022

Dear Diary,

There is a real possibility I could lose her.

Why is no one doing anything?

How long do we have to continue to see her deteriorate, and at what point does her heart rate need to be before they tube-feed her?

Her health is worse than it ever was. I don't know if I should take her to a different hospital. Why is no one listening to me? Why do I feel as if I am being a pain when all I have ever wanted is for her to be well? Is that too much to ask?

Seeing her sitting on her bed so drained of colour, with no sparkle in her eyes, thoughts of losing her flipped something and I needed someone to listen to me; someone to act.

My hands were shaking as I walked into the admin corridor looking for anyone to help. I knocked on the first door I found and poured my heart out to the Deputy Nurse and Head of Safeguarding. For the first time in ages, someone listened and promised that they would investigate and get back to me.

Little did I know that I was about to walk into the lions' den. The next day I was asked to go into the CAMHS room to discuss Poppy. I walked in to find five members of the team waiting for me. My initial feeling of hope faded and was quickly replaced with a need to defend myself. I was told that the problem with me was that if I didn't get the answer that I wanted, I went to another person, but I needed to stick with the plan. Somehow, my cry for help became about me and my failings. I wish that I had called an end to the meeting and rescheduled when I was stronger.

How was it possible that they had turned around my genuine concerns for my daughter's health to blame me? How was that going to help Poppy?

They asked if I trusted them, and my knee-jerk reaction was, "Yeah, I do." However, after pausing for a minute to reflect, I said, "No, not completely." It was only then, by saying it out loud, that I realised that I had lost all confidence in them.

How could I not? My daughter was still starving in their care. I tried to get them to listen, see my concern, see that I just wanted them to keep her safe and reassure me that they would step in, prevent her heart from worsening and that they had a plan to stop her from dying. Was that too much to ask?

I walked away with my confidence in the team in shreds.

A few days later, Poppy messaged to say that her heart had dropped into the 20s, with the lowest reading 24 beats per minute. She asked if she was going to die. I didn't know.

24 beats per minute! How on earth was her heart still functioning? I could hear the stress in her voice, and I promised I would see her soon. Maybe she had got it wrong, so I rang the ward for an update. I was told that they were not able to tell me anything. What on earth? I didn't understand why I wasn't allowed to be updated. I wished they would put themselves in my shoes, hearing alarming news, with no one willing to discuss it.

My determination was in overdrive at the MDT the next day. I needed to know what the next steps were, and I wasn't going to be fobbed off. This was my daughter's life. I asked to see them without Poppy being present. They confirmed what I knew that she had deteriorated, and her heart rate was dangerously low. They expressed their concern that she was the sickest patient on the ward: a high dependency patient. She was no longer able to leave her bed and be wheeled to the toilet, she had to use a commode and was on complete bed rest.

I sighed with relief when they confirmed that they planned to insert a feeding tube that day. At last, they were doing something. I hoped it wasn't too little, too late.

14th March 2022

Dear Diary,

How on earth has this happened? I knew it! How could they not see her deteriorate? How could they do nothing to stop it? They have made me feel like a nuisance and now look what has happened. She is seriously ill, with her life in the balance. This could have been different.

One of my biggest fears is coming true. She could die, and her health has deteriorated in their care. No amount of trying to get them to listen has made any difference.

Why on earth has she been allowed to get to the point where she is the sickest patient? It doesn't take a genius to work out that she should have been tube-fed much sooner.

They want me to visit for only a short time, a few times a week, as they want her to rest and sleep as much as possible. I'll do anything if it means that she will be OK.

Strangely, I am overjoyed yet saddened that she is going to have a nasogastric tube fitted. Maybe this will be the turning point that she desperately needs.

I didn't realise that it would get worse.

When they rang to tell me that they were transferring her to a different hospital, I was instantly relieved as I hadn't been confident about their care.

It made me gasp when I watched her being placed slowly onto the ambulance trolley. Her skeletal body, with a tube inserted in her nose, bore little resemblance to her former self. Her eyes were dull, dark and lacklustre, with all her passion and drive for life replaced by torture and anguish. My gorgeous, caring daughter, who was once full of joy and laughter, was masked, hidden and extremely frightened about what could happen next. She clung tightly to my hand, trying to gain any strength and reassurance that she could.

The half-hour journey to the Intensive Care Unit seemed to drag. I couldn't keep my eyes off the machine, watching her heart rate … 24, 26 … willing it to not go any lower. Each time the alarm went off, I held my breath and looked at the team, trying to read any concern on their faces.

What was to become of Poppy?

We were finally there. So many sounds and beeps from the monitors, tubes, and different smells hit us as we walked into the unit.

I could see Poppy's panic rising whilst the nurse started preparing her feed. She asked endless questions about the feed: "Why am I having this now? How much is there? Why am I having it all?"

They were amazing with her and, in no time at all, she was lying on her bed and the feed had commenced. She couldn't keep her eyes off the feed. Leaving her there was hard but it was refreshing that I was able to ring and visit at any time. I could also sleep by her side, which was so different to the previous hospital.

The doctor looking after her explained that the sudden weight loss whilst in the hospital had caused an electrical imbalance in her heart. She didn't know if Poppy was going to make it as her heart was extremely weak. I was filled with terror. How much could her heart cope with? It had happened too many times.

I had to hold on to hope, that's all I had. I didn't want to consider that she wouldn't be OK. I tried not to think too much about the fact that they didn't know if she would come through. I could lose her.

It was the third time her heart had been affected. Being in Intensive Care made it more real. Could her heart cope with going through it again?

My fear was mixed with anger. I was angry at the previous hospital. Why had they allowed her to get to this point? Although being angry wasn't going to help me or Poppy, it was hard not to be. She needed me as she was terrified that she would die, and it was a real possibility.

This hospital was clear with Poppy from the offset that nutrition was non-negotiable. They had a no-nonsense approach which was great to hear. It comforted me to know that they had things in hand. The initial amount of liquid food was small due to the risk of refeeding, and by monitoring her blood for any impact on her body they were able to adjust the amount.

53

This might be it

I can't lie to you, things were bleak. They kept saying that she might not survive.

I wasn't sure if she would make it out alive.

Her heart rate had never been that low.

I dreaded seeing the doctor, as she said the same thing each time Poppy's heart was dangerously weak, that they didn't know if she would come out of it. There was a real chance her heart could give up.

I didn't want to hear that.

I wanted to hear that she was going to be OK.

I wanted to hear that she was improving.

I wanted to hear that she was out of danger.

I needed to see her each day. I was scared that it might be the last time. I knew I wouldn't be able to live with myself if I hadn't been there for her.

Each day I told her how much I loved her.

The thought of losing her was unbearable.

54

Turning point

I am not sure what the turning point was.

I thought I would continue to be in a state of panic and worry but, instead, I managed to find an inner calm. Something told me that she was going to be OK. I couldn't explain it, but I believed that she was meant to get through it and was going to survive. Each day was another day closer to her getting stronger and I hoped that she could hold on.

I felt confident with the new team as they knew what they were doing. She was finally getting the nutrition her body desperately needed. There was no compromise, and it was happening. Maybe that fuelled my belief that she was going to make it. I would have been kidding myself if I said there wasn't a part of me that was worried. Of course, there was, but my inner cheerleader was in fine flow and was there, in front, shouting that it would all be OK.

Poppy was frightened that she could die. It scared her when she saw staff rushing around to attend to the children when their alarms went off. They were amazing and went out of their way to make her feel more relaxed. I am grateful for the compassion and care they showed us.

She didn't say anything at the time, but I could see that she needed me there all the time. I was fortunate that I was able to work from the hospital, which worked well, and she felt happier with me being there. It made the days long, but it was worth it as I didn't know if she was going to pull through. Recently she commented that she was relieved that I was there, as she had needed me. My message stayed the same, "I will always be there."

My mum hadn't seen Poppy for some time, as due to the Covid restrictions she was not allowed to visit. It was a lovely surprise for Poppy when we both turned up. I admired my mum's determination, as her mobility had worsened and getting in and out of the car was difficult for her, but she put that aside to see Poppy. It was such an emotional time seeing them together. They were both frail for different reasons. My mum was coming to the end of her life and Poppy was close to joining her but I hoped that she was showing signs of fighting back. It was a much-needed boost for them both.

A little while later, her brother also surprised her with a visit. It was heart-warming to see their smiles. Some moments feel right when we all come together, and nothing else matters. It was one of those times, when all the troubles seemed to be a distant memory.

Poppy's heart rate remained dangerously low, and they warned me that it would take some time to improve. Over the following few days, it began to creep up into the 30s, although it was worse at night, still in the 20s.

Hearing that her heart rate was no longer in the 20s was amazing. Although we were not out of the woods, we were heading in the right direction. The biggest difference was her mindset as she had found an inner strength. She wanted to recover and be free of the illness; she wanted to live her life.

I found it hard not to be cynical. Was it the ED talking? Trying to trick us again, to get her home so that she could restart the restricting? I wanted to believe her, but I had been duped so many times. Was this going to be another one of those times?

Poppy described it as having a surge of drive and determination for life. I hadn't heard her say that before. She didn't feel dead anymore. Maybe, just maybe, it could be the turning point that she needed. I wanted it to be. Even she was surprised at how motivated she was to turn it around. This was all new to me, as I was used to the polar opposite, and things had taken a complete 360-degree turn.

I didn't expect that. I loved hearing about all her hopes and dreams, and what she wanted to achieve. It was as if she had a new lease of life. Bring it on Poppy!

Her body was responding, and her stats were heading the right way. I knew it. I knew she was going to be OK. She was going to get through it.

Visiting times became something to look forward to. We were more relaxed, chatting and giggling, just like old times. I found that my motivation and enthusiasm were also lifted.

I caught myself smiling more.

55

A spark in her

The wobbles still came, and the ED voice still tormented her but, somehow, she had gained enough strength to withstand it. It was as if she had a new fight in her. I didn't know how or why it happened, but I was glad to see a spark in her.

She found that being on a continuous feed by a tube, from her nose to her tummy, gave her a rest from the mental torture she was used to enduring.

The next step was for her to start eating something. That scared her, as having a feeding tube took the focus off what she was eating and enabled her to focus on getting through the day. Now she had to do both.

They explored with her what she felt she could do. It didn't matter what it was or how little she ate; it would be a step in the right direction. Despite the voice, the anxiety and the fear, she found the courage to pick up the spoon and start to eat. I was so proud of her.

To be expected, the ED went crazy and placed so much guilt and shame on her for eating. It belittled and ridiculed her, trying to convince her that she didn't need the tube feed, despite only having breakfast. Over the next few days, she increased her eating gradually, but the more she ate, the louder the ED got, particularly when the remaining meal was fed through the tube.

By the end of the second week, changes were happening. It was amazing to see that her eyes were no longer dull and dark; they began to sparkle. I thought I was imagining it and didn't quite believe it until the doctor commented on it too. Her skin was no longer grey, the harshness of her features began to diminish, and the prominence of her bones softened. Great news, her heart also continued to improve.

She wanted to silence the ED thoughts and eat everything, rather than be tube-fed, but the staff tried to persuade her against it, preferring her to ease her body slowly into eating. Poppy was adamant she wanted to at least try, as her desire to remove the tube was strong, and she desperately wanted to reduce the misery that the ED gave her about having to use the tube. She ate nearly everything but, as predicted, her tummy become painful, and she had to rest from eating.

The ED was more vocal, calling out, "You are fat, you are greedy, you have already eaten, you don't need any more food." It was relentless and excruciating for her when the feed recommenced, to the extent that she felt that the only option for her was to eat everything. So that is what she did. She ate everything.

Her heart rate and blood pressure continued to improve, and she would soon be moved out of Intensive Care and back to the other hospital.

56

Mothers' Day

Poppy always puts so much thought into birthdays and Mothers' Day. Last year she was in a unit for Mothers' Day. Unfortunately, this year she was in the Intensive Care Unit and my mum was poorly. I wanted to make the day special and memorable for everyone, as it may have been the last one when we were all together.

Poppy surprised us both. She had put a lot of time into making the day nice for us both. She made a bouquet from paper and card, hand-painted a vase for my mum and decorated the cards herself.

Those few hours we had together formed a great memory that will stay with me; seeing Poppy and my mum in wheelchairs, smiling whilst they raced down the corridors, giggling and pulling silly faces for the camera.

It was lovely to see Poppy and her brother chatting away with, seemingly, no care in the world.

Wow, what a difference a few days can make. What a difference the right nutrition can make. One of the best Mothers' Days I have had. Thanks, Poppy. Thanks, everyone.

What will next Mothers' Day bring? Hopefully, nothing to do with the ED.

57

The only way is up!

It had been two days since Poppy had left the Intensive Care Unit and was back in the same General Paediatric ward. I felt for her, as being there brought back a lot of bad memories. I tried to reassure her that she is in a different place than when she left, and that she could make better memories.

She reassured me and told me that she needed to hit rock bottom and go into the Intensive Care Unit. For the first time, she was able to see clearly how destructive and controlling the eating disorder was and how fragile her life had become, as a result. She needed to see it all. I wanted to shout back that I didn't need to see it, I had already seen the impact that it was having on her. I didn't.

It's hard not to be sceptical. Was she just saying that so she could go home quickly and restart restricting, or did she truly see how close she came to dying? I wanted to believe that she wanted to turn her life around. I tried to hide my scepticism by focusing on being supportive and positive. Yet, I still watched and waited to see what would happen. I clung to it, not sure if it was hope, an inner belief, or maybe a bit of naivety that this might be the time that she would do it.

I knew she could, I just didn't know when it would happen.

I hadn't heard, or seen her, so excited in a long time. They were allowing her to go home for a couple of hours. We wanted to surprise everyone, so we kept it a secret. It felt surreal going out of the hospital with her, driving home together, and her walking into the house. I tried to absorb the precious time we all had together, remembering the smiles and the laughter. It seemed likely that she would be home soon, as her heart was doing better, and she was eating well. She still needed to use the wheelchair as her walking and activity had to be kept to a minimum, but it was only a matter of time before her body got stronger to allow her to do this.

How quickly things changed.

At the next MDT, I expected a conversation about arranging more home leave. I wasn't expecting to hear that her heart had got worse, that they were really worried again, and that the compensatory behaviours had worsened. She had only been back in the ward for three days! In that time, she was back on bed rest, had lost weight, and was being wheeled to the toilet again. What on earth had happened? How frustrating and demoralising for her.

The dietician mentioned that she wanted to see Poppy in two days. I had to speak up. I didn't think waiting two more days was in Poppy's best interests. Her nutritional intake needed to be increased that day, not wait another two days. I'm not sure where my assertiveness came from. It may have been due to my lack of confidence in the team, or my emotions still running high after being so close to losing her. I wasn't prepared to sit there and wait for them to do something. Luckily, they agreed, and they arranged for the dietician to see Poppy that day.

She was inconsolable. She felt that she had taken one step forward and more than two back. She sobbed and sobbed. It didn't help that the Intensive Care Unit had mentioned that when she came back to the ward, she would soon be on home leave. That seemed so far away again. She was no longer able to go outside, and it felt that any freedom she had gained had been robbed as quickly as it had come. She wished that she had stayed in the other hospital, as they had listened to her and were more empathetic. I tried to reassure her that it was only temporary until her body was stronger and that we had to be guided by her body. I tried to reassure myself, but I also wished that she could have stayed there. I hid my reservations from her and concentrated on where we were at. Home leave was paused, which was hard for Poppy as she had had a taste of being at home and no one knew when that would happen again.

Poppy messaged, "Sorry Mum, I was in a dark place and I pulled my tube out." I didn't respond straight away. I couldn't. I was too scared. Scared that it meant she was going backwards. The Intensive Care Unit had always ensured that the nutritional intake was non-negotiable but, unfortunately, that message wasn't the same in this ward and it didn't have a good track record of ensuring that Poppy had eaten everything on her meal plan. That worried me. I saw the tube as a guarantee that she was getting the right amount of nutrition and I was back to hoping that she would eat everything on her plan.

Poppy was so angry with the staff. They threatened that if she didn't eat everything, they would resort to using the tube. The message was the same in both hospitals, but how it was delivered was different; one delivered it in a supportive and encouraging way, the other more threatening and consequential. They were not used to dealing with people being tube-fed.

Poppy said that eating with the NG tube was uncomfortable and she didn't want to go backwards and have it fitted again. It was great to hear that she was using that as a motivator to eat.

It was strange seeing her without the tube, as I had gotten used to seeing it as a part of her. I was concerned that it would be a backward step. However, she amazed me. She ate everything they gave her, every meal, every snack. Every day she did it.

58

Mum, I have something to tell you…

Hearing the words, "Mum, I have something to tell you," filled me with dread.

My head would scream, "Oh no, what's happened now? Has she been restricting, hiding food, exercising?"

"Mum, I don't want this life anymore", she said.

59

Poppy, I have something to tell you …

I see you.
I see the person you are behind the ED.

I see the fear, the worry and the distress.

I see that it has robbed your life of so much.

But that's not who you are.

I see you

I see how painful it is to push against the thoughts and push through the fear and shame.

I see that there are days when you want to give up. It is too uncomfortable for you to keep going,

I see you are scared to leave the comfort and security that the ED has manipulated you to see.

But that's not who you are.

I see you.

I see the amazing fighter you are.

I see your strength, your fire and your resilience, no matter how hidden they are under the thoughts.

I see that you can beat this and create a life you deserve without any rules or constraints.

That's who I see.

That's who you are.

60

Is this the last time?

One of the first things she said to me when I picked her up for her home leave, was that she was thinking of asking the MDT if she could maintain her weight. My eyes filled up and my heart sank. She still didn't get that she had nearly died. Would she ever?

Realistically, I knew that recovery would be a long process, so I was unsure why I thought that it would be any different. She had only been in critical care for a few weeks so, of course, she was still poorly, and was still going to have ED thoughts.

Part of me didn't want to accept it. It had been nearly two years and I didn't want it to carry on. I had tasted freedom and loved it. I wanted more but the reality was that I wouldn't be able to walk the dog when I wanted to, and no longer be able to nip to the shops for some milk. She would need to be watched and supported throughout the day and night.

I couldn't admit it, for fear of being judged, but I didn't feel ready for her to come home. I was afraid in case I couldn't cope with the distress, the arguments, the lies, the manipulation, the deceit and all the pressure that the ED brought.

I was surprised to hear that she felt in a different place, she had a new inner drive and wanted to get her life back. I loved hearing her say that she didn't want that life anymore.

61

Timid mouse turns into a lion

I have found myself in the trap of comparing and feeling envious of other people's lives, quickly followed by feelings of guilt.

It took me a while to accept that they are normal thoughts and don't make me a bad person. They just show that I am struggling with my situation.

Maybe you do the same and wish that life would be easier. I still wish that Poppy would turn the corner and that her life would start to flourish. I also wish that my mum's health would improve. Poppy has the gift to make this happen, but it is unlikely for my mum as she is under palliative care, and we don't know how long she has left.

My mum has always been my rock. Always been there for me, no matter what. Not having her in my life is going to be hard to get my head around and, for selfish reasons, I don't want to let her go. I want her to be there so I can tell her about my day. I want to be able to share the highs and the lows. I want her to still be a part of our lives. Seeing her body getting weaker and tired of being in this world, is hard. There are days when she doesn't want to be like this anymore and wants to take her final breath. I needed her to hold on until Poppy came home so that we could all spend time together.

I was wondering if I could leave Poppy to support my mum, as I didn't trust leaving her on her own, even for a short time. Telling me couldn't have been easy, but she had admitted to waking early to exercise and needing to carry out a specific exercise routine each day. I was worried that the ED would push her to do that again. Being forewarned meant that I could put things in place to break the habit, such as arranging for her to sleep in my room.

Poppy was adamant that she wanted to come home. The referral for a specialist unit (Tier 4) bed was in place if needed. When she was discharged from the unit, her eating was better, but it came at a price. Her self-esteem was crushed to a level that I had never seen before. She ate so that she could come home, which I had been told could happen. Unfortunately, there doesn't seem to be a different model of care available, it's either home or a specialist bed, with nothing in the middle.

How do you know whether they need a specialist bed or can do it at home? If she needed the specialist, let's do it. I just hoped that somehow a balance could be achieved, so she could spend some time with her gran, who had played a huge role in Poppy's life, especially when she lost her dad.

Seeing her gran was a big driver for Poppy to come home. I wasn't expecting Poppy to say, "Mum, I have told CAMHS that I want to come home for a week, next week". I panicked. A week. She had only been home for two hours twice that week, and that didn't include meals. Arghhhhh! How was I going to manage? How was I going to support Poppy being at home for a week? How was I going to care for and spend time with my mum? How was I going to ensure that the ED didn't take hold again? I didn't know.

I wish I had handled the conversation better, but my face said it all. I didn't want the ED to shout and tell her, "Even your mum doesn't want you."

That was not the case. My emotions were high from replaying what my mum had recently said to me about wanting to go to sleep and not wake up. Life felt cruel. Seeing your loved one deteriorate was beyond heartbreaking and the feeling of helplessness was overwhelming.

I couldn't fix my mum's health and I felt that I was being selfish. She was tired, she didn't want to fight or suffer anymore, and she didn't want to be here anymore. I wanted to keep her for as long as I could, but at what cost to her? Whether I wanted her to stay or go wasn't in my hands. I tried to make each day count and spend as much time as I could, making memories for me and the kids.

It hit me in waves, not knowing if she would still be here or well enough when Poppy came home. There was a good chance that I was going to be alone without her in that fight. I didn't have a good track record as the ED has won so many times. I needed every person I could have on my team and one of the main players was leaving, but not by choice.

For it to work at home this time, things had to be different. I didn't know what that difference would be, as some of it had to come from Poppy. I could change how I was, I could support Poppy with the meals, and I could try to prevent the ED having too much space in our household. We needed a life outside it, we needed to grab our lives with both hands, and why not make today 'Day One' rather than one day?

Forgive me for repeating myself but sometimes doing this can help me to make those changes. If I want different outcomes, I have to do things differently.

Home seemed the better option for Poppy and CAMHS saw it as a test to see if she could manage there. This seemed sensible and the Tier 4 referral was kept open. I asked them to explore different support options so that we could have the best chance of working at home. I had a fight on my hands, but their approach was 'one size fits all' and there was nothing else they could offer. We all have different needs, so surely that needs to be reflected in the available treatment.

I was tired of fighting against the system to look at how they could support Poppy, fighting to get through the day, fighting against the ED: it was beyond weary.

I felt that I was the bad guy, being a pain to the people who were supporting Poppy. I was ensuring that I got the best care to keep her safe, which isn't wrong, and I would do it all over again. Maybe this is you too, and you are fighting your loved one's corner. Please know that you are doing your best. I applaud you. Keep going.

I was worn out and a good friend of mine, Debbie, came to support me at the meetings. She was a great strength, empowering me to stand up for what I believed. She had my back and would be my voice when I was too emotional to speak. The difference it made was amazing.

I went from being a little timid mouse, feeling as if no one was listening and sweeping what I had to say under the carpet, to feeling stronger and more assertive.

My inner lion was released and I loved it. I loved not caring what they thought of me. I loved being able to challenge with kindness. I always did it with kindness.

Poppy's panic attacks restarted. Maybe a combination of soon going home, working herself up to see the dietician, and seeing her body change and feel differently.

I was not sure why the MDT thought it would be a good idea to extend Poppy's time at home from two hours twice a week to a whole week and expect it to happen that day. They hadn't considered that I would need to seek work's approval for annual leave, that Poppy had not yet had meals or even slept one night at home, or that I would have to be a carer for both her and my mum.

I was not sure why CAMHS didn't seem to understand the situation I was in as things were different since her last discharge. I had no sick leave left, I was working full-time, I had recently split from a relationship, and had caring responsibilities for my mum. So much had changed.

I began to doubt that I could do it all. But I had no choice. I had to. I felt pressured by CAMHS and Poppy. She was desperate to come home and the team wanted to see if she could manage at home. Sink or swim came to mind.

I asked them to explore options. Maybe an outreach service, a bit like a halfway house, somewhere in between home and Tier 4. They made a lot of excuses. Surely it would have been better for support to be in place?

22nd May 2022

Dear Diary,

Poppy was discharged from the hospital. Yeah! (closely followed by gulp!)

Today was a mixture of emotions. I'm glad to have her home yet have slight trepidation about what lies ahead.

I'm sad that she has had another 10 weeks of not being able to live like a teenager. 10 weeks when the ED has controlled her life and 10 weeks of 'pure and utter hell' which is how she described it.

What is ahead of her for the next 10 weeks? I wish I knew.

Let's hope that this is the last time.

Poppy was overcome with anxiety. As much as she hated being in the hospital, and desperately wanted to come home but, just like previous times, it had been her safety blanket whereas, and now that had gone, there was just us, me and her, fighting the ED.

She needed me to be consistent, supportive, and strong. It scared her when she noticed the small changes to her body and saw that the prominence of her ribs and the discomfort of her spine when she lay flat, were slowly diminishing. Immediately, she wanted to restrict herself as she wanted to see her ribs again. She craved comfort and, when she restricted herself, the ED used the voice of an ally to listen to when the world was putting her under pressure.

I am not sure how she did it, but she used her inner strength and pushed back. She attributes this to being transferred to the Intensive Care Unit and, to this day, believes that the staff there saved her life. It was only then that her drive to recovery came back, bigger than ever. She couldn't explain why or where it had come from. It seemed to come out of nowhere. But it came.

My world felt complete with all of us together - my son, my mum, my daughter and my little scruff ball, Emmie.

62

Caring for two

Getting an early phone call is never a good thing. My mum had fallen at home and couldn't get up. I didn't have time to think about what I was going to see, as we raced around as quickly as we could. The amount of blood hit me. The bathroom floor, the carpet, the furniture, the bedding and her clothes were all smeared with blood stains. She lay on the floor in a fragile heap. Her former self was replaced by a frail body, with her skin covered in cuts and bruises from her fall. It broke my heart to see that all her energy and fight had been extinguished.

I was too busy to think about the impact it had on Poppy and her brother. My instinct was to get Mum back to bed and attend to her wounds as quickly as I could. Whilst waiting for an ambulance, I looked around and saw the worry on their faces. This was their gran, and they were scared. Luckily, she was shaken but OK.

Mum's confidence plummeted and she feared falling again. Over the next few days, her health deteriorated, and the sickness worsened. No medication seemed to ease it and I was concerned about how little food she was eating.

It happened so gradually. A little sleep here and there, increasing to longer periods. It then became more noticeable, as her words slurred, her sleeping increased, and conversations were harder as she would fall asleep within seconds.

Instead of trying to enjoy the last few weeks, months, or however long I had left with my mum, I was stuck in a cycle of constantly scrutinising and feeling responsible for how much she was eating. I didn't want to nag her or focus on food in another relationship. I didn't want to be the bad guy again, ensuring that she ate enough to survive, but it was hard to watch another loved one slowly fade away, barely surviving on 500 calories a day. I was surrounded by eating issues. Poppy was battling with her ED, and my mum was barely eating due to the nausea.

She spent more time in bed, her skin became more fragile, and regular inspections took place to check for pressure sores. I thought it was the end and the nurse confirmed that she probably didn't have long to live; maybe days, possibly weeks. I wasn't sure how I was going to tell my kids. What impact would it have on Poppy? She was fragile and I was worried that it would set her back. The nurse helped me break the news to Poppy, but hearing someone else say the words brought it home. I wasn't ready to lose my mum. I don't think we are ever ready to lose someone we love.

Our focus soon shifted to keeping her comfortable and spending as much time as we could with her. I was so grateful that my brother came up that afternoon, as it helped me, knowing that someone else was there.

I was barely coping with caring for one. Caring for two required energy I didn't have. How was I going to balance looking after them both?

63

Happy Birthday to me

It was my birthday. It's been a long-standing joke with family and friends that, each year, I turn 27. When I was younger, my dad would insist that he was 27 again and again. Silly, I know, but it has stuck with me. Even to the point where I find myself forgetting how old I am, much to my friends' amusement.

It was a lovely surprise to come downstairs and find the house decorated with streamers and banners. Seeing the huge 2 and 7 balloons made me chuckle. They had both put a lot of thought into making it special for me.

The pamper session that I had booked was just what I needed. It was slightly clouded as I worried about leaving Poppy, but there was something different about her. She seems more focused on her recovery this time. People asked me how she was doing, and I still couldn't bring myself to say it aloud in case I was wrong, and she relapsed. I found myself crossing my fingers when I answered, as I used to do when I was younger, hoping that everything would be OK. Something inside me told me that this was not necessary as she genuinely seemed to have a strong desire to get her life back and step out of the cave she had been living in for so long.

I found myself reflecting on my life and where I was at. I know I am not 27, maybe a little older, alright maybe even 20 years older (shh, don't tell anyone). I get asked if I fear getting old. No, I haven't given it much thought. People say age is just a number, and it is, but this year it felt different. As much as I tried, I couldn't brush off the thought that it might be the last birthday I spent with my mum. It is hard to hear how tired and fed up she is. Seeing someone slowly fade away can make you question your life.

It hit me suddenly that the little monster was in fine form. It was nagging in my head, asking me, "What have you done with your life? What have you achieved? What are you going to do over the next year to make it count?"

I felt deflated, upset even. What had I achieved, what had I done with my life? At first glance, nothing at all, but who says I haven't achieved enough? Who says I haven't done enough? Who says I must do more? No one does, just me, so why was I feeling like that?

I could only see the difficulties, the impossible times and the heartache. It was too easy to focus on the negatives: what I hadn't achieved, what was missing, and what I wanted, rather than what I had done or what I had.

That was not how I wanted my birthday to be. I was allowing the negative chatter to dampen my day. It was time to kick it into touch. It was time to switch it. I had an idea.

I would often say to Poppy, "Let's switch it."

It's time to heed my own advice. I allowed myself to wallow for five minutes, to listen to the negativity, to dwell on all the things that I felt I was missing out on. I was fed up with not being able to do simple things, such as going out for afternoon tea. Mum was too poorly to go and Poppy was not in that stage of recovery to be able to do it yet.

I remembered the previous birthdays when the ED was very much present. Two years ago, Poppy was entrenched in the illness, the distress was so immense that she was barely eating, her body so thin, and no amount of encouragement or persuasion could get her to eat anything, there was no chance that she would even consider eating birthday cake. A week later, she had been admitted to the hospital. It is impossible to enjoy your birthday when you are frightened of what the future holds for your daughter.

A year ago, the ED was still a constant figure in her life, when she had been at home for two months from the specialist unit. She was so determined to make it a lovely day that she pushed herself and managed to eat a little piece of cake. However, the distress, guilt and shame she felt afterwards were debilitating. I had felt robbed. I wanted one birthday where the ED was not invited, one birthday where she could eat cake in a carefree way, and one birthday where she was free from all the rules.

The alarm I set for five minutes was a reminder that the wallowing time was over. It was time to switch it and look for the positives. Reading the birthday messages helped squash the chatter and brought me back to the present. I have achieved so much over the last few years. The biggest achievement has to be that Poppy was alive and still fighting. I have been there every step of the way to support her. I have fought and will keep fighting. I have survived the last two years. I am not the same person I once was, I have grown, and learnt more about myself in the last two years than in the last forty-plus years. I recognise that I am strong and resilient. I have achieved so much.

It was time to enjoy the rest of our day and the outdoors, something that would always lift me. During the first part of our walk, I was back in the negativity. I could feel my eyes fill up, a lump form in my throat, and pity engulf me like sudden darkness. I shed tears for all the things that I wanted to be different. I wanted my mum to be well again, Poppy to be back to her usual self and all of us to enjoy time together. I knew that it was not helping me and that I was too focused on what I hadn't got.

"Come on Emma," my cheerleader bellowed, "You have a choice on how the rest of your day goes, so let's make it a good one!"

I stretched out my hand to Poppy and we walked the rest of the way, hand in hand. The anger, frustration and upset slowly disappeared. I chose to see the positive: family, love, togetherness, closeness and so much more.

It was a lovely afternoon in the end. I was able to enjoy the scenery, and a particular highlight was Poppy and me, laughing at our dog, trying to chase the leaves as they blew in the wind. I couldn't resist popping into the local gallery and treating myself to a silver bracelet. I am not one for a lot of jewellery, but it caught my eye. It was simple, delicate and unusual. "It is my birthday, after all." I told myself. "Everyone deserves a little treat now and then."

Poppy surprised me and topped it all off by making the most amazing video. Unknown to me, she had contacted several friends and they had sent video messages for her to compile. Another reason for my tears to flow, but it was a happy reason.

I had a desperate need to soak up the time with Mum so I could remember the memories we had with fondness. She had been too exhausted on her birthday and her presents had remained unopened. My birthday was as good a time as any to change that. It made it more special for me, with us both opening our presents together. I had lost sight of how lucky I was to have so many great friends and family in my life.

It might not have been the birthday that I had hoped for but, in the end, it was just right, with the right mix of family, friends, love, giggles, a few tears and lots of hugs and smiles.

No amount of birthday wishes would have done better.

64

Cherish the moments

One piece of advice I was given was, "Enjoy the moments that you have together."

I didn't see how I could, at first, as I was often too entrenched in looking at what was going wrong. I came to recognise that I enjoyed the time we had played games and cards and watched movies together in the hospital. Reconnecting was precious to me.

Each day, or at the end of each week, I would reflect on some of the moments that we had together. It might be something as small as a smile, a shared giggle together, playing card games, or chatting as we went for our walk with the dog.

Just like before, Poppy's activity levels needed to be kept at a minimum to allow her body to adjust to being at home. By using my mum's wheelchair, we gained freedom and no longer needed to be stuck indoors.

I was apprehensive when I took Poppy to London on my coach training weekend. She had only been discharged two weeks before then, but having the wheelchair made such a difference and we were able to do so much. The musical show was amazing and the sun was glorious as we walked around the park.

Going home wasn't as smooth and hitting the rush hour proved a challenge to catching our train, with only four minutes to spare.

Imagine a crowded train station and you spot a woman sprinting as fast as her little legs can go. A girl in the wheelchair is being thrown sideways as they dodge the many obstacles and people in their way. She urges the woman to go faster, with a grin on her face. She runs to the lift, quickly presses the button and you can see them both mouth, "Come on, come on." She runs in with the wheelchair and they look at their watches. The woman mouths, "We are not going to make it, we only have two minutes." But the girl responds, "We can, we can." The other passengers in the lift let them exit first as they can see the urgency. You have never seen such speed. She could beat the world record hands down, as she legs it along the platform and narrowly manages to board the train, with the wheelchair, before it departs.

That was us, with a few seconds to spare. Poppy couldn't stop laughing, as she was giggling at what the people said to us in the lift, "You can make it, you have two minutes, you can do it." I flopped into my seat, dishevelled, hot and sweaty; certainly not looking my best, but I didn't care. We had made it and Wow! what a weekend, what fun we had had and what great memories we had made.

Cherish the moments that you have, no matter how big or small. It helped me in those testing times to look for any positive fun times.

I invite you to think about what has gone well over the last few days or the last few weeks, or maybe something that you have enjoyed or giggled about, or where you had some time for yourself, no matter how short. Keep looking for those times, as they will remind you that there are often some good moments even in a difficult situation.

65

A fresh start

Poppy saw the new school term as a fresh start. We had few months to get her stronger, both physically and mentally, before school started.

I pushed CAMHS for a robust discharge plan, as she needed the right support and tools. What it looked like I didn't know. They were the experts, not me. I wasn't backing down this time and she needed support.

Whilst stabilising her heart rate and weight was a priority, it was like putting on a sticky plaster. I wanted to prevent it from happening again.

What would make the difference to her? It was like taking your car to the garage and, instead of replacing the faulty part, they make a temporary fix but, at some point, that part will cause problems and could cause more damage to the car than if it had been fixed properly in the first instance.

66

Working on self-care

At every appointment I went to, I was referred to as Poppy's mum. That was my identity. I was rarely asked how I was doing and was often forgotten. I hadn't realised that it was exactly what I was doing - forgetting myself.

I would prioritise Poppy whenever I could, neglecting my needs, to the point where I had no time, energy or motivation for self-care. The only self-care I had was looking forward to going to bed.

I had to learn how to prioritise myself but thinking about it made me feel selfish and that it was impossible to find the time.

It is necessary to have some 'me' time away from our struggles. But it may not always be possible. It became a challenge to find the time or a way when I could leave Poppy and my mum.

Some days were better than others.

A good mindfulness tip I was given was, "Whatever you are doing, try and be in the 'here and now'." Instead of juggling many different tasks together, concentrate on one. That was me. To save time, I would often have a drink whilst tidying the kitchen. Now, I sit down and experience the drink, feel myself holding the cup, and notice the taste and the temperature. If I notice my thoughts wandering off, I bring myself back to the experience of drinking. This only takes a few minutes and can be used for many other things. I use it when I brush my teeth. As I focus on the task, I taste the toothpaste, feel the toothbrush in my mouth and notice the smell of the toothpaste.

The more I do this, the easier it is to focus on being in the present moment, helping me to calm my mind in my struggles. Poppy is working on this too and it will, in time, help her to manage her emotions.

67

Finding the positives

In the beginning, I was desperate to help Poppy change her thinking, and encouraged her to find the positive in a situation. I even tried comparing her situation to another awful one, thinking that she would see how good she had it and that would help. It didn't, and I am not surprised it didn't.

We can feel under pressure to be positive and maintain a cheery upbeat outlook. Doing this can hide our feelings and emotions, but it is not possible to be positive all the time. It is OK to feel upset if something hasn't gone our way.

I would often try new techniques that I had read or been advised about. Putting them into practice was not always easy to do, and I often judged myself as a failure. It doesn't help to tell ourselves that we are failures just because something hasn't worked. Accepting how we feel is different from accepting how ineffective it was. We don't have to write it off if it doesn't work, maybe it just needs a tweak and try again.

There will be times, no matter what we say or do, when they will still find it stressful and difficult to eat. That is no reflection on us or the amount of effort we have made, it is more about where they are at with their illness.

When faced with a bad day, it is not always easy to approach things in the best way, but it doesn't mean that we have done something wrong. All that may be needed is to try again or take a break and let someone else take over, if possible. I used to think that was a sign of weakness, but now I see it as a sign of strength, recognising that we need to look after ourselves as that ultimately benefits others.

While looking after someone with an eating disorder, there are often other things or people requiring our time and energy. Combined, they can leave us feeling overwhelmed, anxious or stressed.

Owning and accepting our feelings helps us develop a greater sense of self-power and self-understanding which, in turn, helps us cope better with challenging situations.

Struggles and disappointments can knock us down and crush us, however, we can choose to give up, or learn from them and use them to help us move forward.

I have often been told to slow down as I have two speeds, fast and faster. I rush around, sometimes not realising that is what I am doing. I am working on taking things slowly, but I haven't completely mastered it. I must continue to remind myself that it doesn't matter if the household jobs don't get completed and they can wait for another day or another week. Working out my priorities has helped to relieve some of the pressure.

Have you ever felt 'meh'? That was a new thing for me, where I didn't feel particularly great, and would muddle through each day, lacking the 'oomph' to see things through. By talking with friends, I was able to get things off my chest and often ended up having a much-needed giggle.

Setting small goals each day helped to reset out of the 'meh' time, whilst ensuring that I didn't get into the mentality of holding it against myself if I didn't achieve the goals.

Using grounding techniques was a good help, particularly with Poppy. We both love walking in the woodlands, especially with the dog, and we would pause for a few minutes and answer the following questions.

> What 4 things can we hear?
>
> What 3 things can we see?
>
> What 2 things can we smell?
>
> What 1 thing can we touch?

Walking alongside me was a real struggle for Poppy, as the ED would bully her to walk faster. It is amazing to see the difference a mindful game makes. Her favourite games are:

> How many countries can we name before we get back home?
>
> How many red things can we see?
>
> Name a song title beginning with each letter of the alphabet.

68

What's in your rucksack?

When Poppy was around 2½, she would carry the cutest rucksack with a cartoon character everywhere with her. She would fill it with anything she could find, often to the point where it wouldn't close or was too heavy to carry. She wore it with such pride, even around the house. "Poppy, do we need to take it today?" I would ask and I was always met with, "Yes, Mum!"

Have you ever seen parents or grandparents carrying a child's small rucksack on their shoulder, too small to wear properly, whilst the child runs around playing, carefree? That was me too, as she would tire of carrying it, or it would get in the way of her playing and she would discard it without a moment's hesitation.

The cartoon character soon became uncool and was quickly replaced by a brand new one for school. No longer was the rucksack filled with cuddly toys, games, snacks, her favourite books and anything else that she could find, as water bottles, pens, pencils, and reading books became the main contents. The pride in wearing it was still there.

That rucksack was replaced again, as out went the girlie one and in came the more grown-up one as she moved to secondary school. The number of pens, pencils, and books changed. Some days her back would ache from the number of books she had to carry. The pain was easily relieved by either swapping it to the other shoulder or taking it off completely.

If only it was that easy to carry her emotional rucksack. We all have one as we experience highs and lows in our lives. Every struggle, failed relationship, illness or death of loved ones, and personal or work-related setback, is carried around with us. The amount of baggage we each carry can vary.

Poppy's emotional rucksack was weighing her down. The light, positive fun things were buried way down at the bottom. They were hidden by the loss of her dad, her self-beliefs, hatred for her body, pressure to be perfect, the ED thoughts, guilt and shame, social anxiety, and many more.

She kept stuffing in more and more traumatic times and awful ED thoughts whilst choosing to ignore her feelings. Each battle she faced, each difficult day she experienced, and whenever she felt she wasn't listened to, would be added to the rest.

All this did was add more pressure. The rucksack gradually filled up, subtly getting heavier with neither of us noticing. The weight on her shoulders had become the norm.

She no longer passed me the rucksack; it remained hers. Try as I did to remove it from her, I couldn't. She couldn't just swap it for another one or discard it.

I hadn't realised it, but I had my own emotional rucksack. Mine was also getting heavier with each struggle, each emotion suppressed, and each difficult day experienced. The spiky monster was in its element. It was loud, screaming that I needed to be strong, hide my emotions, cry in private and keep holding on, regardless. Adding more and more to my rucksack. I felt the weight of the world on my shoulders. I was easily irritated, had little or no sense of humour, and couldn't see the fun in anything. It was not a good place to be.

There were many times when it all got too much and instead of my emotions being contained in the rucksack, they would overflow. I would either collapse in a heap, distressed and wanting to leave, or my emotions would fizz over like a bottle of pop. It would occur over an insignificant thing but, to me at the time, it would have been huge.

It was all too much. Either way, I was not the best version of myself, I would often feel out of control. I couldn't keep living like that. But I didn't know how to change, I didn't know how to take the rucksack off.

It was hard to admit to myself and sharing with you is even harder, that I was resentful. Resentful of the life I now had, angry that we were in this position, and wishing that she hadn't started to restrict her food intake. As a parent, that is hard to vocalise, but I know that she didn't do it on purpose and was doing what she could to survive this world.

Buried deep inside was anger. I was angry with myself. Full of regrets that I didn't notice the illness or do enough to prevent or stop it. The load on me was huge and I felt trapped and frustrated that my life had been ripped apart and replaced with continual battles. We were stuck in a vicious cycle, and there seemed no way out.

I was fortunate that Poppy and I had a relationship where she would share her feelings and troubles, but that still didn't help.

I read a lot of books on self-development and positive thinking. They helped a little but nothing changed. It was through writing this book that I came across an amazing lady who introduced me to a book on handling grief.

I wanted to know more, so I enrolled on the course, although I was initially sceptical about how it could help. CAMHS had been focusing on the ED and Poppy's anxiety but not on the loss of her dad, so I wanted to see if this would help.

My focus was my kids, especially Poppy, so I wasn't thinking about myself when I enrolled on the course. As far as I was concerned, I wasn't the one grieving. My dad had died over eighteen years ago and I had accepted that.

The weekly café visits, the cuddling on the sofa watching telly, the day trips, the shopping trips, and holidays without the monstrous ED were all things that I missed. The hopes and dreams I had, now seemed so unachievable. I came to see that I wasn't just missing the life I had lost, I was grieving for it.

That opened my eyes. I had assumed that grief was about losing a loved one, but it is so much more. It is any loss, such as a divorce, losing a job, moving home or a separation.

The course made me see that all emotions are normal. For years, I had been hiding how I felt, especially in front of the kids. Always putting on a brave face, modelling that emotions were good or bad, and should be suppressed. That being angry, frustrated, and upset meant that you were a bad or weak person. That is not true.

It was time to relearn and reset my beliefs. It is OK to cry, to feel angry, frustrated and defeated by life's struggles. When I got things wrong or said the wrong thing, instead of believing that I was a bad person, it gave me a greater insight into questioning myself. Did I intentionally want to upset her, or do anything to impact her? Of course not. There was no intention to hurt or upset her. It didn't mean that I didn't love her or care for her any less. She and my son were my whole world, and I was doing the best I could at the time. It is normal and human to have emotions from daily battles. When Poppy said things that upset me, it didn't mean that she loved me less or intentionally wanted to upset me. We were both doing what we could to get through.

The illness dominated her mind with ED thoughts. There were times when it was impossible for her to stop restricting her food intake, or to stop exercising excessively because she felt fat, even though she was dangerously underweight and her body was weak. Her emotional reasoning drove her perceived reality. I realised that even though, to us, it wasn't true, her truth was that she felt fat and lazy. Dismissing or distracting that, and not listening to how she was feeling, did not change the truth that she believed. She didn't need fixing; she needed to tell me her feelings and needed me to listen, with no interruptions, no judgements and no criticism.

I was able to experience first-hand how it worked, and the results that could be achieved. I felt incredible and lighter. For the first time, I could breathe. I hadn't realised that all the pressures, emotions, struggles, failed relationships, divorce, and job moves over the years had added weight to my rucksack.

It was no longer heavy; it was lightweight and I felt free. A feeling I had not felt in such a long time. The course was the best thing I had done.

I could show my kids that we no longer need to hide our emotions or cry alone. Our emotions don't need to be labelled.

It was time to be a role model, to be open to my feelings, to talk from my heart, and to no longer be afraid or judge myself.

So much good has come out of this course. I am fortunate to have met so many incredible people from different parts of the world, with different experiences and different losses. We refer to ourselves as family and I hope that one day, I will meet them in person. Incredibly, instead of allowing the losses to hold them back, they are using them to help others, which is inspiring. Even though I have felt battered, distraught, and defeated many times, I hold on to the belief that good will come out of this. I have told Poppy that we can either stay down, play the victim card and let that shape the rest of our lives, or we can be proud, honoured, and thrilled to use our experiences to help others. That is exactly what we are working towards.

"Nothing is permanent in this wicked world, not even our troubles."
Charlie Chaplin

69

Happy moments

I loved it.

I had been looking forward to spending time with friends, which I had not been able to do over the last 2½ years. I couldn't wait. Going out for a coffee may not sound exciting but, to me, having a taste of normality was something I desperately craved.

It was like a piece of heaven. Sitting outside in the garden area, soaking up the warm rays of the sun, enjoying the laughter from the ease of conversation, whilst eating a toasted croissant and sipping an ice-cold raspberry lemonade, I wanted to savour that moment for as long as I could.

I felt like me. Not a mum, not a carer... just me. It was heavenly. The place was soon buzzing, as more people arrived. I looked around and I was just like everyone else, having a drink, something to eat and catching up with family and friends. I was not a mum who was fighting against the ED. I was not a daughter who was caring for her mum. For a few hours, I was me. And I loved it.

I was able to detach from everything: the pressure of my potential job loss, the worries of increasing living costs, my mum's health and the scary possibility of Poppy relapsing. Her body dysmorphic disorder (BDD) was a drain. She was at the point where her clothes were getting tighter and this had contributed to her previous relapse. We were uncertain if she could get past this point. Despite the nagging worry about what she would do in my absence, I was able to accept the chatter in my head, yet embrace the conversations, the giggles, and the niceness of it all. It felt not just normal, but a new normal for me. The only downside was it left me wanting more.

I loved how much energy I felt afterwards, with my internal battery fully recharged. I must remind myself that I need moments like those, big or small, it doesn't matter.

70

Life can resemble a mobile phone

I'm not sure what it is about the sunshine, but I love it. It always seems to raise my mood, and everything seems rosier.

It was time to book a summer break. Normally it was something I looked forward to. A break from work commitments and the norm, and an opportunity to see new places and meet new people. It would be our first holiday for over two years, a combination of not being able to travel because of the Covid pandemic restrictions and Poppy being too poorly to travel.

It was difficult to muster any excitement or strength to push past my negative thoughts. It seemed too much trouble to go away. If it wasn't for Poppy being so keen, I would have happily stayed at home.

I felt guilty leaving my mum, as she would have loved to come with us, but was too unwell to travel. I was worried about the impact of the holiday on Poppy. She desperately wanted it to be like the old times. She didn't want any restrictions on the length of time she could walk and she craved a break from the rules coming from her head. She desired to be like everyone else and wanted to enjoy the holiday. Getting a balance was going to be hard as the ED would, no doubt, make its presence known, making it harder for her to relax.

I would hate it if someone told me that I couldn't do this and I couldn't do that, especially on holiday, as it's a chance to get away. But if you have an eating disorder, its suitcase will be packed too and no amount of persuading it not to come will make any difference.

It was uplifting to see her so excited. She adored being by the beach and the sea had a calming influence on her. I was glad we went. I witnessed a new sense of freedom within her and she was able to have some fun, despite the ED being there. My confidence grew as a result.

Poppy spent the summer holidays pushing against the ED, challenging its thoughts, and continuing to work on some of the fear foods, so that she would be in a better place to start sixth form in September. She saw it as a new start. She deserved one.

Going away was exactly what I needed, I felt recharged. Reflecting on the holiday moments made me think that life can sometimes resemble a mobile phone. Bear with me on this, it will soon make sense.

Some days, my energy levels were depleted from the endless battles, daily arguments and upsetting confrontations. The low battery warning sign would come on. Difficulty finding the right charger meant that the phone was barely functioning, and any extra demands would drain the battery and it would be no good to anyone.

With so many different apps available, I spent too much time engrossed in them, worrying about what people think, and too much time listening to the voices in my head saying, "I can't do this. I am not strong enough. When are we going to be free from this?" Scrolling through other people's lives highlighted how bad things were for us. Envious that others were having fun and were free from the constant turmoil, demands and arguments. It reinforced how stuck we were in the ED world, while life passed us by.

Just like the phone, I too can access the storage. I can decide which memories I want to keep or delete, which ones are my favourites and I can make new ones. I can focus on the negative memories and difficult times, or I can focus on the positive moments and the happier times, no matter how small or brief they were.

Regular updates are essential to keep the phone working in good order. I would attend the various Beat sessions and participate in parent groups to keep me updated and fix any bugs and glitches that I had.

The evitable anger and frustration would build up from time to time. I would want to shout and scream, but that didn't help anyone and would break our relationship more. It made her feel lonelier and more isolated and she would turn inwards, towards the ED. I was fed up with feeling stuck where I was a victim, with a lack of control, doing the same thing every day and getting the same outcomes. A reset was needed. Seeing things how they were, enabled me to reset myself. The new wallpaper was showing the words, "Girl! You've got this!" and the lock screen showed, "Go and get those pants on."

Sound familiar? That was me. I was constantly on an emotional rollercoaster, and every moment doing battle used up my energy until I was running on empty. I would regularly deplete myself. I was not performing at my best and was no good to anyone. There was no option though but to carry on. My daughter was reliant on me … my family was reliant on me.

Throughout the journey, I have complained, gotten angry, frustrated, and upset and have focused on what is wrong. I have let it destroy a part of me. By doing the same things, I got the same outcomes.

It has taken me time to see that I have the power to control how I react and respond. I can choose to slip into the old habits of complaining, focusing on the bad parts of my life, feeling as if life has it in for me and playing the victim's role.

As much as I would like one, I don't have a magic wand, but I can try and be a better version today than I was yesterday.

We can control how and when we recharge our batteries.

We can spend time with those that helps us recharge.

We can learn from our mistakes and not beat ourselves up.

We can remind ourselves that we are doing our best.

We can focus on how far we have come.

We can focus on enjoying the time with our loved ones, no matter how short, whilst remembering that this is a temporary situation and won't last forever.

Thinking positive thoughts isn't going to change the situation but it can help to change our perspective. If I want a different outcome, I must do things differently. I need to put my super underwear on, pull them right up and shout out loud, "Knickers to it! Who says I can't?"

Who says I can't pause for a moment?

Who says I can't get through this?

Who says I can't scream and shout when no one is looking?

Who says I can't be a better version of myself today?

Who says my life is over?

Who says we can't beat this?

Who says we can't do this?

Not me! My super pants are on!

I can and will do it ... and you can do it too!

It is OK if you are running on empty or on automatic pilot. I have. If you don't have the energy to put your super underwear on, that's OK too. Some days you need to do what you can for your well-being. Tomorrow is always another day. Another day to be a bit better, to do a bit better than yesterday. If you don't manage it, then that's OK too.

I know that you want to do your best to help. I apologise for saying it again, but it does need saying. To help others, we need to be kind to ourselves and take a break to recharge, and not be afraid to ask for help.

We all need to recharge. On this difficult journey, your loved one needs you. Your family needs you. You need you.

You've got this.

Please do something for yourself today, no matter how small. Chilling in a bath filled with bath bombs and watching a girlie film (whilst trying not to drop my phone ... shh, don't tell my kids) was one of my ways to relax and recharge.

Please do something for yourself today. If not today, then tomorrow. Pencil it in your diary if need be ... but do something.

You are important.

71

Flip it

I took my own advice and booked some time with friends. I didn't enjoy it.

No matter how much I tried to enjoy being with friends, I couldn't shake the anxiety of leaving Poppy for a few hours. No matter how much I tried to keep her safe from harming herself she seemed to find something to use. No matter how much I tried to tell myself that everything was going to be OK, I couldn't always see it.

I was trapped.

Is this going to be my life for the next 2½ years?

Poppy didn't tell me until the next day that she had cut herself. Seeing the multiple wounds, and the exposed fatty tissue, floored me. Despite trying to keep her safe, and despite her brother being there to support her, life was too overwhelming for her. The pressure was relentless: navigating school, mental tiredness, ED thoughts, and pushing through the social anxiety was all too much for her.

It was the first time in a while that I had gone out. I felt selfish. Selfish for wanting a life, selfish for wanting to have some 'me time', and selfish for wanting time away from the worries and troubles that the ED brought.

How could I go out again?

How could I have a life?

How could I go anywhere?

I craved freedom as I was trapped in a world of fighting and supporting Poppy, day in and day out.

The urge to run away was enormous, it was the only thing I could think of. I wanted to run and not look back. I knew it wasn't going to solve anything, the problems were still going to be there. I just wanted us to be free from the pain, free from the misery, and free from the fighting.

I couldn't see the wood for the trees and had been too invested in what I couldn't do and how far we had left to go. Overthinking the details, I had lost the ability again to see the whole picture.

Allowing the emotions to pass, I saw more clearly and I remembered advice from a good friend, Michael Heppell, who showed me how to 'Flip it'.

And that is what I did. No longer was I going to focus on what I couldn't change. I flipped it and focused on what I could change.

My thinking flipped from, "I am trapped and not able to get out" to "For now, this is where I need to be, and I can use this time to complete my course and become an emotional coach." That enabled me to see the opportunities and possibilities that I had in front of me.

I flipped my thinking and realised that Poppy was doing her best to cope. It might not be my way, but it was hers, for now. I couldn't change what had happened, but I could change how I responded and explore how we could manage things differently.

"We are not out of the woods."

Flip it to "We are not out of the woods, yet."

My eyes were still firmly on Poppy, watching for any signs that the ED was taking charge again. When it did, that was my cue to grab my big girl pants and restart the fight. We had the support around us, and we had tools and a map to show us how to get out of the woods; we just had to keep taking the steps to make it happen.

Just like in the woods, we might have come across trees that had fallen in our path, which were too big for us to climb over, causing us to turn around. That didn't mean that we were not going to get out, it just meant that we had to find a different way.

72

My face was smiling

7th September 2022

Dear Diary,

I was taken by surprise. The last few weeks have been hard but today was such a beautiful day. It was lovely seeing Poppy going to school. She looked brighter and more like her old self.

Having a few hours away from the ED was bliss.

I felt great. I was singing away to the music blaring from the radio. Just for a few moments, I didn't have a care in the world.

Everything felt normal.

I felt free.

I revelled in the peace and the calmness.

I loved sitting there, absorbing the warmth of the sun shining through the glass. It seemed to amplify how great I felt. I wanted to bottle it and keep it nearby.

I didn't want it to end although I knew it would. I knew as soon as Poppy came home, reality would kick in and I would remember that I am an ED mum, fighting to win.

I was bathing in it for as long as I could. I noticed that my face was smiling and my body was relaxed and calm. I loved it.

Here is a message to you, ED. I am fully recharged and raring to go. Look out!

73

New start

There is something so beautiful about autumn with the explosion of colour as the leaves prepare to fall. It's one of my favourite seasons. It's a great reminder that changes are not bad, and sometimes we need to shed our old habits, thinking and beliefs, and welcome a new beginning with new opportunities.

Seeing her smile on her first school day was rewarding. Maybe, just maybe, it was the new start she needed.

No sooner had I thought this, I could see that she was hiding behind her smile. She hid the sadness, the pain, the anxiety and the fear. The pressures she faced were too much for her. As much as she tried, it didn't take long before the smile began to slip.

The ED was relentless, pushing her to restrict herself, encouraging her to exercise, and not allowing her to relax. She felt out of control. Previously, she would have defaulted to restricting her eating. This time, she held onto the knowledge that, if she listened to the ED, her life would contain endless days stuck in the hospital, having to go through the pain of eating again, weekly MDTs and having to gain weight, not being able to come home, missing her family and friends, a tiring reset of the vicious loop she couldn't seem to get out of. That wasn't the life she wanted.

Each day she became more tired as the pressure continued to build, amplified by her inability to rest, and her need to do extra work intensified as a way to cope. Her schoolwork consumed her life and there was no room for any fun. No wonder she felt overwhelmed and exhausted.

In a short time, she was out of control again. She was like a runaway train heading for a collision and she couldn't get free from the internal pressure she put on herself. The train had to be stopped and the brakes had to be applied to prevent a collision. It looked likely that Poppy was going to have to either reduce the number of subjects she was studying or have time away from school. She refused point-blank as the thought of not being able to go to university at the same time as everyone else meant that she was a failure.

Despite everyone's best intentions, she continued to head for impact. The estimated time of arrival and the damage was unknown. It was 'all or nothing' thinking for her, only failure and success, with nothing in between. The more out of control she felt, the more she felt a need to cope in any way possible.

She lost quite a bit of weight. I think I had been waiting for that to happen. I thought she would revert to her ED ways sooner, especially as the pressure was beginning to be too much for her.

She admitted what I already knew deep down. She had been restricting; not to lose weight, but she was finding a way to cope. I told her that I didn't care what she got for her exams, I didn't care if she didn't go to university; all I cared about was that she was happy and healthy. But she cared, she cared too much.

Just as before, it started a little bit here and a little bit there, restricting her food. The impact on her body didn't happen straight away which made her think that it was OK and that she could get away with it. So she continued, ever so discretely, when she could. She enjoyed the peace of restriction, no matter how small it was. She continued to remove food until the game was up, and it became clear to see.

Previously, I would have blamed myself for not seeing it happen, and catastrophizing that we are back to square one. Instead, I saw it for what it was, it was a blip, and she had resorted to her default way to cope.

It was time to get back on the right track.

It was time to get on our 'Let's do this' underwear.

Poppy instantly saw herself as a failure and felt she had failed me. That was not true. She is human, so we will have times when we go back to our old ways. For some of us, our old ways do not put our lives in danger. Hers do.

I told her that I was proud that she had told me, that it was not a sign of failure, it was strength, bravery and courage, all great qualities of someone who recognises that it doesn't have to be that way and, working together, we can get back on the right track.

As hard as it was for Poppy, she knew that my involvement was to be more hands-on for a while until she could resume the place where she was the sole driver of her train. I sat alongside her, helping to steer and recheck the direction so that we would avoid any collisions and reach our destination.

Poppy continued to lose weight despite two meal increases. I knew something wasn't right but I couldn't put my finger on it. When questioned, she whispered that she had included the weight of the bowl when weighing her food.

I felt stupid. I couldn't believe that I had missed it. I hadn't given it any thought that she would do that.

After admitting that, the guilt, shame and sense of failure engulfed her. She knew that the next day would be different. She would have to eat everything, and she knew that she would suffer from her ED thoughts.

I was pleased that she had told me and I knew what I needed to do.

We are taking each meal, each snack, each day as it comes so that I can be assured that she is having the right amount. It is calming for me that I can do something and not just sit on the wings, waiting and watching.

Poppy could see that she had been stuck for some time with her ED thoughts, unable to push forward with her fear foods and see a way out.

She described it as holding onto the edge of a cliff with all her might. With each meal, each day, she became more exhausted and could feel her grip loosening. Some days she could muster just enough strength to hold on, and others she was barely holding on. She didn't know how much longer she could.

I was not surprised that she found herself wanting to let go, it seemed the only option to her. She saw the ED as part of her; no longer was she Poppy, she was Poppy with an eating disorder, and she didn't know who she was without it. When life was hard, she felt it was easier to go back to what she knew, to have the comfort, the safety blanket that the ED could bring. It was scarier to push forward against the pain, and into the unknown. Seeing it that way, helped me to use it to connect with her, as I was able to validate how she was feeling.

She was able to see that something had to change. She had two options. Let go and tumble down, probably to another hospital admission, or use the help and the tools to find a way out so that she could get a glimpse of how life could be.

Each day I asked her what was the one thing she looked forward to doing that day: possibly watching an episode online, reading a book or listening to some music. The only condition was that it had to be something for her.

We continued to work on finding the middle ground with her school studies with her school studies so that she had time to do other things and experience a little freedom, and a little joy in her life. I have been doing the same, finding something each day that I enjoy, even if it's just for a few minutes.

74

100 is the magic number

I have asked myself so many times:

Why can't she let go?

Why can't she see what it is doing to herself?

Why can't she see that she nearly died and not just once?

Why does she keep running back to it?

Knowing the impact that the illness can have helped me understand the whys. I still didn't like them but at least I understood better.

Poppy's anorexia led to malnutrition, which affected the way her brain worked. It caused the brain to shrink, with the neurotransmitters and emotional centres also affected.

I was aware that her hunger cues had stopped, which made eating more difficult. I also noticed that her cognition was affected, making it impossible, at times, for her to think and remember.

Her recent food restriction had affected her weight and, without the right nutrition, it was likely that it would continue to affect her brain. The good news is that when someone recovers, so can their brain. A key part of this is weight restoration and nutritional rehabilitation, or as I say to Poppy. "Food is medicine and food is non-negotiable." She hates hearing that. I wish it was that simple but it's not and, unfortunately, no single treatment can cure the illness.

Ensuring Poppy had everything on her meal plan was, on some days, impossible. Trying to get her to see the plan as a minimum was unthinkable.

Once, she was measuring out her food and suddenly froze, staring at her bowl. I'm not sure why I did it but I put on a high-pitched voice and started to role-play.

"It's 101 grams. Oh, no! I have to take out a grain of rice. Which one should I take? Which one is the heaviest? Is it this one? Is it that one? Nah, maybe it's that one. It can't possibly be 101 grams. It needs to be 100. Oh, no, the world is going to end if it's 101 grams."

I looked at Poppy hesitantly. She smiled and put her hands on her hips, waving her finger at me. She looked over the rim of my glasses which she was now wearing, just like a teacher about to tell her student off and, in a silly voice, she said, "It's 98 grams. Come on Poppy, a little more. It needs to be 100 grams. Oh, no, you can't leave it at 98, can't possibly leave it at 99, must be 100, what are you thinking? 100 is the magic number."

We both were in hysterics, and she left the scale measuring 101 grams.

It may seem strange to quibble about a gram or two, but the more Poppy can push past her fears, of having more than her meal plan, the more she can free herself. The next step would be to stop weighing the food. When there is a period of weight loss we would then go back to weighing for a little while, just to make sure that she is getting what she needs to stabilise her weight.

It wouldn't matter what it was; a grain of rice, a segment of orange or an almond, but Poppy couldn't bring herself to eat outside her meal plan. It took a trip to Wales to give Poppy the push which made the impossible possible.

She realised that if she wanted to see the beauty of the coastland, she had to take the first step, she had to fuel the walk. And she did. She loved standing on the top of the cliffs, watching the waves hit the rocks below, and enjoying how the wind felt against her face. She raised her hands triumphantly in the air feeling a rush of freedom, strength and newfound determination.

That day was such a powerful day for her. Whilst she still remembers the internal battle that she had to overcome, she also remembers that that was the point where she was able to take her first step.

Being by the sea seems to bring out the best in Poppy, as it offers her a glimmer of hope that she can come through this. I try to remind her of this, just like I remind myself of the good times.

She needs that too.

75

Winning the lottery

Being the upbeat one is tiresome.

Seeing the mental pain, day in and day out, etched across your loved one's face is tiresome.

The ED, still being present in our life, is tiresome.

It was difficult to shake off the need to be ever-watchful for what seemed to be 24 hours a day, 7 days a week. I was on constant alert, searching for evidence if she was hiding food, being extra vigilant to keep her safe, and on my guard to check that she was not exercising or stockpiling medication. No wonder I was exhausted.

I sometimes let my imagination run away with me and wondered what my life would be like without the illness. Have you ever imagined yourself winning the lottery? Yet, instead of winning money, my lottery win would be for the illness not to have started in the first place. That would be worth more to me than any amount of money.

No longer would the ED be a constant feature in our lives.

No longer would our conversations be consumed by the illness.

No longer would Poppy be ruled by her ED thoughts.

The odds of winning the lottery are slim. Some days, the odds of Poppy winning her life back also seem slim.

If someone had told me that I would endure this battle for more than 2½ years, I wouldn't have believed them.

Unfortunately, many do not fully recover. I try to focus on those who won the lottery and got to live their lives.

This train of thought raised the question, "What is winning in life?"

Is it winning the lottery?

Is it avoiding mistakes?

Is it never having to feel hardship again?

Is it playing it safe?

Is it having a smoother life?

I often find myself dreaming of a life where everything goes smoothly, and there is no hardness, pain or struggles. It would be great, especially at the moment, but these are unrealistic expectations. Life is not like that.

I used to think that I was losing in life. With Poppy nearly dying, my relationship breaking down, the loss of our old lives, Groundhog Day with the same daily turmoil, the same struggles and the relentless pain they brought. It took me time to see that life is a mixture of moments when, at times, you feel like you are winning and, other times, like you are losing. Just like Poppy, I often found myself overwhelmed.

For too long, I had defined the 'win' incorrectly. For too long, I had allowed myself to sabotage my hopes and dreams and, for too long, I had listened to the spiky monster inside me.

This journey helped me look at my life with fresh eyes, and I saw that the possibilities were endless. I was able to see my 'wins' clearly: our family were closer, we had met a lot of lovely people and, despite everything, I never gave up. I have grown and developed as a person, I have worked on my beliefs and learnt to listen to my fluffy cheerleader. I am now doing things that I would only ever have dreamt of: training to be an emotional coach, writing a book, and helping others who are going through this journey.

I see now that there are moments in our lives where we feel we are losing, failing, and hitting rock bottom … call it what you like, are part of life. It doesn't mean that we are not winning. How we define 'win' is the important thing, and this means different things to different people.

All the losses, struggles and challenges on the journey that we have gone through have made me the person that I am today.

Wow, that sounds like I am winning. I know in time that Poppy will find her own 'win' and I can't wait to share the lottery with her.

76

Recovery is possible

I have heard people say that recovery is possible. Despite my wavering hope at times, I know it is true.

What is not made so clear, is that recovery is painful, with little or no respite. It is no wonder that our loved ones are often exhausted, frustrated, scared, angry and fed up. Who wouldn't be?

Watching your loved one go through this while knowing that you can't take their pain away, is difficult to endure. I will never know the full extent of Poppy's pain. So often, I wished that I could step into her shoes for a day or take her pain away so that she could recharge to get through it, but I couldn't.

What I could do was keep feeding and nurturing her, being there to listen and cuddle her when times were tough. I could remind her of what life could be like and share that I believed she could do this. That recovery was worth it and all those tough times would pass, and when they did she would be glad that she kept going.

For so long, I thought of the ED as a monster and that her mind was broken in some way and that she needed to be fixed. However, I came to realise that she is a normal person, she was not broken, and there was no monster inside her. It was her way of trying to survive.

Coming to this realisation, helped me to see Poppy in a different light. She was the same girl that I loved, my lovely daughter, Poppy. She had been doing her best to protect herself and, in time, she would see that she no longer needed that level of protection.

I wholeheartedly believe that Poppy will get there, and the Dialectical Behaviour Therapy (DBT) that Poppy is having will give her tools and techniques to help with her emotions.

In time we will no longer be stuck in the woods, we will be able to enjoy the scenery.

I recognise that there will still be some days when Poppy will walk slightly ahead of me in the woods, or on her own with guidance, and others where I will need to walk alongside her.

This won't be forever, it's just for now.

77

Aha moments

Mum, I feel I have more energy.

Mum, I feel more refreshed.

Mum, I feel less cold.

After two days of not restricting, Poppy was noticing the difference. It was a no-brainer to me, but not to her as she wasn't well enough to see the impact the restriction was having on her body.

At the height of the illness, she was afraid of many things, such as shampoo, facewash, handwash and even toothpaste. She couldn't bring herself to smell, or touch, her food for fear of absorbing calories. I hadn't noticed as this was often masked by the other battles we were facing.

Now, Poppy can smile, and even laugh, at how bizarre her thinking was.

There are many rules and rituals that she is still submerged in. Sitting is still a massive challenge for her, as her mind and body go into overload and her only respite is to stand. We have been using the graded exposure approach, so every day Poppy sits on the settee for a short time. When her body screams with pain, she holds the urge to stand for a few more seconds. The key is consistency and starting small, even if it's just 30 seconds for 1-2 weeks.

We have also been using this approach with her fear foods, introducing one or two pieces of white pasta each time until, eventually, she can eat a plateful. This is not the only approach available and some parents find it better to 'rip the Band-aid off' and expose their loved one to the plate of white pasta in one meal.

No two days through this journey have been the same. Challenging fear foods and rules is scary and, some days, Poppy will eat the food with no problem but, on others, I catch her reducing her food intake. Sometimes she is in an emotional spiral and needs a lot of reassurance and support.

This can be such an upsetting, emotional and mentally draining time. I would like to share some of the things I used to say to myself to maintain the compassion, empathy, and consistency that Poppy needed.

★ If I don't get it right all the time, that's OK. I am doing my best.

★ She is not well. The eating disorder is driving her anxiety and fear.

★ She is frightened and this triggers her flight and fright responses. It's going to take her some time to move out of this response.

★ Validate how she is feeling, so that she feels listened to and less alone.

★ If needed, take some time out.

With time, patience and consistency she will overcome the rules and rituals.

I look forward to watching them disappear, one at a time.

78

Green shoots

I have experienced many highs and lows throughout this journey. It still fluctuates between the two, but now the lows don't last as long and I have the insight to know what I can do to help.

Although Poppy was often buried deeply under the pressure and ED thoughts, she has always been there, needing help. The ED can be all-consuming to everyone involved, so remembering the joyful moments helped us to keep on slaying the ED.

There might be days when you too will have a glimmer of hope. There might even be brief moments when you have glimpses of your child. Use these to remind yourself that better days and better moments can happen. Perhaps reflect on this at the end of each day, or maybe at the end of each week; whatever works for you, so that you can see some of the sunshine through the horrendous thunderstorm.

These are the green shoots of a plant and, with the right nutrients and conditions, they will grow slowly and, in time, will blossom for all to see.

79

What do you want your story to look like?

When you look back on your life, do you want a story full of regrets? Or one which says, "See what I accomplished" and shows the impact you had on others, the memories you made and the love and kindness you showed?

I want that story. It might not seem like it right now, but my purpose is to help my daughter so that she can rewrite her story. I am a key character in her life now, but I will hand that role over to her so that she can be the star. I will sit in the wings and enter the stage when I am needed, and I will be her biggest cheerleader.

I have focused on learning throughout this journey, through the coaching, learning about myself, learning to be more empathic and how to truly listen to her. I am a better person now than at the beginning.

You might feel like me, that you are not in charge of your story. But, like me, you are one of the VIPs in your loved one's story. Right now, you need to be centre stage. You might switch from playing the baddie who gets booed and has food thrown at them, to the goodie that saves the day. It may be that you are playing the baddie for a long time, but that is your role right now. It won't be all the time and you will get cast in a different role where you are the headliner, and you can decide who you want to be.

This wasn't the story I wanted my daughter to star in. Who would? Stories can be rewritten at any point. We can choose how to show up; whether we want the experience to hold us back or allow us to grow. Our lives will never be the same and there will always be that 'thing' in the back of my mind, as I watch out for any signs that the ED is taking centre stage again.

I am embracing this new life and the new bond that we have. My daughter didn't die, and I am so grateful that she wasn't another statistic. My heart goes out to anyone who has lost a loved one.

I used to believe that Poppy was in recovery but came to recognise that she had been kidding herself, and me, and was more likely in recovery to relapse. We are now further forward in her recovery, and I am hoping that this time, she is in recovery to recover.

This reminded me of being a young girl when I loved a happily-ever-after, be it a book or a film. As I got older those happily-ever-afters were not the same. There was no one to rescue me, and not everything worked out the way I wanted it, and the perfect life that I craved is a pretence. Despite this, I still prefer a film where everything works out in the end.

When I first started writing this book, I imagined that this would be us, sharing our happily-ever-after with you and giving you hope that you can get through this too.

What I have come to realise is that this happily-ever-after can be whatever we want it to be. It can be me instilling the belief and resilience that no matter what the ED throws at us, we will overcome it.

Just like where a book or film ends on a cliff-hanger and you want to know what happens next, that is where Poppy and I find ourselves. We need to star in a happily-ever-after sequel and slay the ED. It may take a few sequels, but it will happen.

The ED cannot beat a mother's love.

80

I won't throw in the towel

I have great news to share with you. My mum is still with us. She is not out of the woods yet, but we have seen some improvements. Like Poppy, she is made of strong stuff. Perhaps sheer stubbornness. I'm not sure which.

It must be a family thing.

I would love to tell you that Poppy is back on track.

I would love to tell you that she is finally free of this cruel illness.

I would love to tell you that we are both doing great.

Unfortunately, no to all the above.

Recently I discovered leftover food in her lunchbox. It was not a huge amount but enough to trigger an alarm bell that she was struggling and that I needed to step in and take the lead. Despite the initial protests, she replaced the food that she hadn't eaten. That was a huge thing for her to do and reinforced that the meal plan was non-negotiable, and every mouthful was necessary.

My underwear had to be dusted off to regrow the thick skin required to deflect the moans, groans and anger that came from the ED part of Poppy. She was uncomfortable having me watch over her meals again. It helped that I acknowledged her feelings and said that, whether she felt anger or frustration, anyone else would feel like that in her shoes. It helped her to know that I understood that it wasn't aimed at me, but it was the situation. It would have been too easy for her to default into feeling she was an awful daughter and a horrible person.

I am prepared to step in and meet her for lunch, pull her out of school, and reduce her activity levels if necessary. There will be pushback, but I can't let her deteriorate again. I'm not sure that her heart would cope with the strain.

We continue to work on stabilising her weight, as one week she loses and the next she gains. Any increase is difficult for Poppy as the ED thoughts are vile, and a lot is centred around her fear that CAMHS will make her fat. No doubt, she will be tempted to find a way to restrict calories somehow, but I am standing strong, watching her like a hawk. I think she is eating everything, but I say that with trepidation, as the ED is so sneaky, and it's hard to be 100% sure.

The CAMHS meeting brought it home to me. I was determined not to cry but I couldn't stop my eyes from filling up when they said to Poppy that they were sorry that she had had to endure the illness for such a long time, and she probably couldn't remember a time when she thought or felt differently. There was no stopping the tears when they mentioned how stuck she must be feeling and that it was a cruel illness. On her way home, Poppy repeated that she couldn't do it and didn't want to do it anymore.

We spoke about her two options. Give up or get up, but either way, we had to go through it. Neither option is easy. To give up meant going back to the hospital, restarting, and being back in the same position. To get up we would find a way through together, to enable her to get to where she wanted. To do her A-levels, to go to university, then travel and see the world with her friends.

That night she sent me a message, "I want to do it, Mum. I really want to. Can you help me?" I wanted to jump for joy.

Despite the odd moment where I want to throw in the towel, there is nothing more uplifting than seeing that fight in her.

The journey ahead isn't going to be easy. There will be moments when she doesn't want to let go of the ED life, fearing what she will be like without it, and not being able to cope with changes in her body size. There are still moments, and will be for some time, when she doesn't want to eat or wants to restrict herself. My answers are always the same; eating is non-negotiable and remember your why – why are you doing this?

Poppy's why is that she wants to go on a school trip abroad for two weeks, which will be an amazing experience. CAMHS and school are working together to make this happen. It is going to take a lot of work and planning so that she is physically well and can eat the food she needs when she is there. They continue to develop a toolkit to support her mental health should she need them. The use of placemats, whiteboards and motivational quotes are helping to keep Poppy focused on her goals and a reminder of her why, so she can ask herself, 'Will this help? Will restricting this food help me achieve my goal?".

CAMHS hope that this will be the driving force for Poppy to push through the ED thoughts, and to encourage her to step out of the cave she is in.

So, I won't throw in the towel. Not today, not tomorrow. I don't expect her to realise it now, but one day she will be glad that neither of us threw in the towel because she will have slain the monster.

81

A Christmas miracle

Christmas has changed for me over the years. From relishing the time when Poppy and her brother believed in the Christmas magic, with the experiences of visiting Santa and enjoying the school nativities and Christmas carol services.

Christmas is very different now. Gone is the childlike belief but it is replaced by the magic of togetherness and fun.

I love the build-up to Christmas. I love the feeling that I am a child again, taking in the sights as we walk around and see the houses displaying their lovely outside decorations and the beautiful lights twinkling to the warmth and kindness witnessed in others. It really can feel like a magical time.

It was our third Christmas with the ED, but I was determined that this year, it would not take the magic away for Poppy. It was a hard balance, embracing the festive activities but not letting her overdo it so that she would lose weight.

As a special treat, we went to a night-time light show on Christmas Eve, which was beautiful, and there was so much to see and do. Poppy loved it. However, it was sad to see that, in the background, the ED was trying to rob her of enjoyment. She was plagued with thoughts of how much extra food she needed for this walk, which ultimately led to disagreements and tarnished the experience.

Having my mum around for Christmas Day made mine. We didn't think it would happen, and we were amazed and thankful that she was still with us.

It felt like old times, seeing the joy on the kids' faces as they opened their presents, and the spills of laughter as we ran around after the dog to stop her from opening any more presents. But it wasn't like old times, as there was a palpable air of sadness in Poppy. The ED was still present and took some of the shine from the day.

What Poppy did was, in my eyes, a Christmas miracle. She sat down! She sat on the settee, not on her knees, not standing up but sat down, and played on a games console with her brother. That was the best present I could have had. And she was enjoying herself, just like the old times. She had pushed past the ED thoughts, pushed past the pain in her body and remained sitting. Wow! And double wow!

But I should have seen it coming. It was inevitable. It was all too much for her and she broke down. I held back my tears, as I hated seeing her like that. I thought I was prepared but it was too much for me too, and I felt angry and bitter that our day had to end like that. Poppy needed me but, right then, I needed me, so I told her that I was struggling with my emotions and needed time out.

I wasn't expecting it to be a perfect day. I knew that there would be challenges and some difficult moments, but I knew that there would also be some happy times, and that is exactly what we had. That is what I reminded Poppy of, as I thanked her for such a lovely day, and for being so thoughtful with her gifts, especially the cute doughnut ornament she bought for the tree. It was a great reminder that, no matter what difficult times we have, we will always come through. I asked her to see the day for what it was; us sharing time and having some fun.

The next day, I grabbed a green bow, one that you stick on presents, and placed it on Poppy's head. Her expression said it all, "Mum has lost the plot." I explained that she and her brother were the best presents that I have ever had and that I was so proud of them both.

I can't wait until next Christmas.

82

That belly laugh

The next day after Christmas, I was looking around the house. The kids' presents were still downstairs, with the odd bit of wrapping paper on the floor. The house needed a bit of a tidy-up, the washing was getting out of control, and it was time to do the many jobs that I had been putting off.

I'm not sure how it happened.

"Oh, no," I cried out.

"What is it, Mum?" Poppy asked.

I showed her and she started to giggle. She looked at my face and tried hard to stifle her laughter. She failed and continued to giggle, with her eyes glistening. I groaned and had to look twice. Maybe it wasn't that bad.

It was.

I stood, pathetically holding up a wet, grey, diamanté jumper, with the words 'Winter Wonderland' glued on the front. The arms, the width and the length were all too small for me and would have probably fit a 9-year-old child.

Poppy continued to giggle. I held it up for her to see, desperately trying to stretch it. Maybe if I put it on, that might do it. Nah, I can't get my arm in, let alone my head. That didn't work.

She continued to giggle, pointing at the sleeves and highlighting how tiny they were. I held back a giggle, as it seemed disrespectful of my jumper to join in. I found it hard to hide the disappointment of accidentally ruining my favourite, and most expensive, jumper. I loved that jumper, as I instantly felt great when I put it on.

Her brother walked in and asked, "What's wrong?"

I reluctantly held up the jumper. He looked at Poppy, then at me, before starting to smirk. All the while, I was tugging and stretching, trying to make it a bit bigger. I looked down but there was no progress; no amount of stretching was going to make any difference.

My kids were laughing, that belly laugh that makes your eyes water and your tummy hurt. It probably didn't help that, each time they looked at me, I was still looking in disbelief that I had shrunk my favourite jumper, or maybe it was the way I was trying, with all my might, to stretch it.

In between the giggles, they suggested that I put it in cold water to see if that would reverse it. As I walked into the kitchen, they let out the laughter they had been trying to hold back.

My poor jumper no longer fitted me. Did it matter? Nah, not really. What mattered was seeing my kids giggling together at my expense, something they did when they were younger. It was heart-warming to see them do it again.

You never know what your day will bring.

You never know what is going to happen to make you smile.

You never know how many memories you can make without the ED being present.

83

Striking the underdog

I still find it impossible not be wounded by the pain I witness in Poppy. After our first CAMHS appointment in the New Year, she whispered that she was done, with nothing to live for, and no fight left. It cut me like a knife to see her expressionless face, her stooped posture and dull eyes. I was scared that she would end it all.

I didn't want to lose her, and I especially didn't want to lose her to this illness.

I reminded her of her passions for life, of all the places that she wanted to go. Anything that I could think of to ignite a flicker of hope in her. It was hard to tell if it helped. I felt as if I was treading on eggshells for the rest of the day and did not want to add extra pressure, which would be the final domino to bring it all come crashing down.

I could no longer hold in my emotions. I flopped on the carpet and cried for her pain. I cried for the life that she was stuck in and for the pain that I knew was ahead.

It didn't seem great timing that Poppy had an appointment with her therapist that afternoon, but it did help. There was a noticeable shift and the dark cloud seemed to have, somehow, lightened and become smaller and more manageable. The fear of gaining weight and the ED's pressure were still there, but no longer did I need to tread with trepidation.

"Come on, Poppy, which one do you want?" I asked.

"I will go with the underdog," she answered, as she choose the smaller baguette.

"On your marks, ready," I shouted.

With a cushion in one hand and half a baguette in the other, we took turns to strike and see whose baguette would break first. Emmie was loving it, jumping up and down, trying her hardest to grab any crumbs.

The baguettes held on. We giggled.

Another whack and a small crack appeared on mine. She giggled.

My turn and Poppy's soon began to crack. "No!" she cried. I couldn't stop giggling and had to cross my legs. At my age, you can't be too careful.

Is it cheating or tactical thinking to hold on, covering the slight crack? With surprising force, she whacked my baguette and hers flopped to the ground, defeated like a stale leftover to be thrown in the bin.

No sooner had I shouted, "Defeated!" than Emmie took the opportunity to bound as fast as she could and grabbed the discarded baguette. Much to her disappointment, we prised it off her, but we did give her a doggy biscuit as a consolation prize.

It had been a stressful start to the day and, despite the silliness and laughter, the suicidal thoughts remain and will be present in varying intensity for some time which, unfortunately, is part of the illness.

But where I can, I will continue to bring a bit of silliness, a bit of fun and some much needed time out from the ED in our lives.

I hope that you can too, no matter how small.

84

New Year's reflections

A New Year can bring a lot of pressure to become a 'new you' and make the year better than the last by sticking to your New Year's resolutions.

It can be a triggering time for those with eating disorders as there are often conversations about losing weight and how much food has been eaten over the holiday period, not forgetting the bombardment of diet adverts this time of year.

It is too easy to get swept along with this and focus of what you have not achieved, how difficult the previous year was and what you should have done instead. There is that 'should' word again. It is not helpful and if there is one thing I can do this year it is to drop that word.

I have been reflecting on one person I haven't considered until now. Poppy's brother, Jordan, her older sibling by three years, and the impact of all this on him.

He has not only seen his sister shrink in size, but he has also seen her close to dying. He has witnessed the outbursts and distress, and has seen the scars of the battles. He has seen me in all the different shades of laughter, tears, frustration, to wanting to give up and yet finding the determination to keep going.

I have never once heard him complain.

He has been insightful, recognising that, at times, she would rather die than eat. What impact this must have had on him, I think in time I will find out.

He has always been there for her, and for me.

Sometimes, it takes situations like this to see how amazing a person has become, right under my nose.

In time, he will get his sister back and they will experience joy again. I will enjoy watching in the wings when this happens, just like the old times.

85

I found a way

I found a way to stop her restricting.

I found a way to stop her cheating on weighing days.

I found a way to stop her exercising.

I found a way not to give up.

I found a way to become an emotional coach.

I found a way to keep my hope and belief alive.

I found a way to keep her safe.

I found a way to motivate her.

I found a way to listen when she wanted to give up.

I found a way.

No matter what happened to us, I always found a way.

Like the unexpected doughnut thrown at me, life can be the same. No one knows what it will throw at you. Everything can be going smoothly and then, in the blink of an eye, your world has been turned upside down. I certainly hadn't expected to be on this journey.

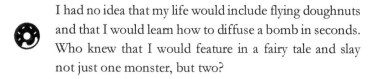

I had no idea that my life would include flying doughnuts and that I would learn how to diffuse a bomb in seconds. Who knew that I would feature in a fairy tale and slay not just one monster, but two?

I may still have to keep dodging the odd doughnut.

I may have days when the ED has little, or no impact, and other days when I may find myself stuck, covered in jam from head to toe, feeling a mess, and unsure how to unstick myself.

But no matter what each day will bring, I know I will find a way. And so will you.

86

Thankful. Really?

I never thought I would say this, but I am thankful for this journey.

I didn't think this every day, but it's true. I am grateful. It seems a strange thing to say when I look at how devastating it has been for all of us.

For many years, I felt as though I was walking around with a blindfold on. Now the blindfold has fallen, my eyes are open to a world of possibilities and opportunities.

As surreal as it sounds, I can see clearly for the first time. My perspective has changed, on how I interact with my children, my mum, my friends, and other people I come across. My learning has been massive. My beliefs have been reset. I feel lighter and closer to my family. I have been fortunate to meet so many lovely people who now have a very special place in my heart.

If it hadn't happened, I would still be the person I was, whereas I have discovered more about who I am in the last 2½ years than in the previous 40 years. I have developed a character of strength, faith, belief, courage, resilience and much more, some of which I never knew possible. It seems bizarre to thank my daughter, but without her going through this, I would still be doing the same thing, with the same perspective, getting the same outcomes. And yes, I thought I was happy, but I can see now that I was just getting through each day.

There were times when I didn't like myself for what I said, or how I reacted. I wasn't always the person that I wanted to be. Some days I had to fight myself to see the joy.

But that is being human, as we don't always get it right, and we don't always say or do the right thing, but that's OK. I don't need to be perfect. Perfection is overrated.

Whereas, now I see that I am not just an ordinary mum. I am Emma, an extraordinary warrior who is strong, compassionate, caring, loving, kind, determined and capable of so much more. That is who I am.

I want to ask you, my dear friend. Who are you?

Maybe you're an ED sufferer.

Maybe you're a parent or carer, supporting a loved one.

Maybe you're fighting a different struggle and think there is nothing special about you. Just like I did.

I can wholeheartedly say that each one of us is incredible. We all have amazing qualities and capabilities that make us who we are.

We might not see them, but they are waiting to be dusted off and shown to the world.

We all offer something special to the world. We are not ordinary.

We are extraordinary.

87

To Anorexia

To Anorexia,

This would be much easier to write if you were a real person.

I didn't see you sneak up on us.

I didn't see you twist your way into her life.

I didn't see you manipulate her, every way you could, until it was too late.

You have robbed my daughter of so much; her smiles, her hopes, her dreams, and her zest for life and, at times, mine too. You have stripped her of her identity, her self-worth and, nearly, her life. She has endured such pain, having to crawl her way out of the black holes, only to be sucked back into your mindset. Like a hamster on a wheel, she was unable to get off or break free.

I see the pain that you cause her.

I see the light that you have taken from her.

I see the cruelty of what you are doing to her.

She is scared of letting you go, exhausted by the pain and turmoil that is ahead. She has moments of clarity when she wants you gone, then other moments when she can't imagine who she would be without you.

She doesn't see you for what you are, your use of bullying tactics to get what you want. You ridicule, belittle and degrade but, when needed, throw in some praise and comfort to lure her back. Yet she still stays with you. If you were a real person, I would have rushed around to where you live, I would have packed her bags and done everything I could so that you would never see her again. The problem is that I cannot see you, but I know that you are there.

You are there every day, at every meal and at every snack.

I pull one way and you pull the other. I manage to free her a little, only for you to circle around and draw her in tighter. I ramp up the effort to overcome you, only to find that you have outsmarted me. I am hit with the reality of not getting very far as I fall flat on my face. At times, I have felt broken, defeated and exhausted from the endless battles and have been so desperate for it to end, that I have wanted to run away.

But I don't.

No matter how many times I have fallen, I have found a way to rise again.

I will keep rising to fight for my daughter.

I will keep supporting, encouraging, and walking alongside her.

I will keep doing what I can so that she sees you for what you are.

I used to think of you as an invading monster, slowly destroying my daughter, but I now see that this has been a way for Poppy to cope with the world.

In time, she will see that too. She will see that she no longer needs you, no longer needs to be frightened of food, and no longer needs to be held back by her ED thoughts.

In time she will develop her identity and you will be nowhere near.

Your time will come to an end, maybe not today, maybe not tomorrow, but someday soon.

And that, Anorexia, is a promise. A mother's promise.

Emma

88

Poppy, you will rock this world

I cannot finish this book without writing to my beautiful Poppy,

Dearest Poppy,

I wouldn't be a parent if I didn't embarrass you.

I make no apologies for saying how amazing you are. You are beautiful, both inside and outside, compassionate, loving, thoughtful and incredibly kind. I mustn't forget to mention that you are a tight pants too. I bet you are shaking your head reading this. Have I embarrassed you enough?

You are an incredible daughter and I am a very proud mum. Never forget that, Poppet.

I'm aware that there have been times when you have felt like the worst daughter ever and have hated yourself for the things that have been said and done. Each time I knew that it was the illness talking.

There were times when I wished that it never happened. Maybe I would have got there on my own, or maybe I would have kept walking through life in black and white.

This journey has opened my eyes to new beginnings and possibilities. I have said goodbye to old beliefs and old ways and have welcomed new ways into my life. I have learnt a lot about myself, good and bad, all of which have helped me to create a new direction and purpose in life. I will always be grateful.

I know that you are beginning to see things differently, and in time you will have a different life from the one you have now. The blackness you find yourself in will evaporate, and wonderful colours will flourish within you.

Poppy, my darling, I have always believed that you will come through this and that so much good will come out of it for you. I didn't expect that it would be that way for me too.

I am looking forward to hearing about your school trip and seeing the photos.

I am looking forward to your book launch and seeing your book in print when you tell your story, as a teenager living with an eating disorder.

I am looking forward to seeing you beat this illness.

You will rock this world, so go and grab your boxing gloves.

 Get back in the ring and let's get punching.

 You have a fight to finish, one that you will win.

 Go, Poppy, go!

Love you loads and loads, Mum xxxxxxx

89

You can get through this

I want to thank you, from the bottom of my heart, for sharing this journey with me.

I wish you and your loved ones strength, hope, stamina and a sense of humour for whatever life throws at you. You can get through this.

No matter how tough the battle is, how many of your battleships are sinking, or how many doughnuts you must dodge. You can get through this.

If you take anything from our journey together, please remember that when you are exhausted and fed up, take some time out for yourself, no matter how little. You can get through this.

When it all seems impossible and you feel that there is no way out, flip your thinking. You can get through this.

Dust off your underwear. Find the right pair for you, the one with the superpower that you need to get through the challenges ahead. You can get through this.

Go, grab them. Pull them up high and wear them with pride. You can get through this.

Don't forget that:

You are amazing.

You are a warrior.

You are stronger than you think.

You, my dear friend, have got this.

All the very best of luck to you and your loved one.

Take care and I'll see you at the summit.

With all my love, Emma xxx

I would love to hear from you, so please get in touch:

emmacarterwriter@gmail.com

Helpful contacts

I would like to share a selection of contacts, books and websites which provide great support and information as we navigate our way through this illness.

SEED	Support and Empathy for people with Eating Disorders Support Services
Email:	support@seed.charity
Telephone:	01482 421525
Website:	seed.charity
Beat	www.beateatingdisorders.org.uk
Eating disorder support	www.eatingdisorderssupport.co.uk
First Steps ED	www.firststepsed.co.uk
FEAST	www.feast-ed.org

Books:

Hope Virgo	'Stand Tall Little Girl: Facing up to anorexia'
	A great social media account to follow.
Eva Musby	'Anorexia and other eating disorders, how to help your child eat well and stay well' Her website contains helpful information.

Emma Woolf	'An apple a day: A memoir of love and recovery from anorexia'
Harriet Brown	'Brave girl eating'
Nikki Grahame	'Fragile: The true story of my lifelong battle with anorexia'
Tabitha Farrar	'Rehabilitate, Rewire, Recover! Anorexia recovery for the determined adult'
Lauren Muhlheim	'When your teen has an eating disorder: Practical strategies to help your teen recover from anorexia, bulimia, and binge eating'

Parent guide:

'Skills-based caring for a loved one with an eating disorder: the New Maudsley Method' by Janet Treasure ,Grainne Smith and Anna Crane

Acknowledgements

I am blessed and grateful to have so many wonderful people in my life who have helped and, when needed, pushed me to make this book happen.

I want to thank Poppy from the bottom of my heart. She has patiently listened to me reading the chapters. She knew I would write this book and her belief in me has never faltered. Poppy, I did it. Now it's your turn.

To my mum, I can't thank you enough for being there as a sounding board when times were tough, and I couldn't see a way through.

To my brother, your support and phone calls have been so valuable in helping me to keep going. Thank you.

To Michael Heppell, I am grateful for your support and enthusiasm, as you encourage me to write that booooooooook!

To all the amazing Write that Book members for your help and guidance. Particularly, I want to thank Deborah, Nia and Ruth, as our regular catch-ups inspired me to keep writing; Sarah and Eleanor, your advice was amazing; and Matt, I couldn't have done without your typesetting skills, bringing it all together.

To the lovely Christine for your editing skills and giving me that final push to press send, and to Jenn for putting up with my many suggestions to tweak the book cover. I love it. To

Rob, thank you for helping with the website, and saving me from having a lot of headaches.

To Debbie, where would I have been without you standing alongside me? You are one in a million.

To Linda, I am grateful that our paths crossed. You are an absolute warrior. Our daughters will come through this, and I hope that we will meet one day.

To Dawn, I'm not sure what I would have done without our walks, as they gave me much-needed time out to vent and cry. We always ended up laughing at something.

To Helen, I loved our catch-ups. We always found something to smile about, and I was recharged by your compassion, understanding and enthusiasm for life.

To John and the Shalom Men Fellowship (Christian men), a big thank you for your thoughts and prayers for Poppy and my mum. You comforted us during the difficult and scary times we faced. One day, I hope that Poppy and I will be able to thank you all in person.

To Marg, thank you for taking time to write the foreword, and a big thank you to the amazing team at Seed Eating Disorders Support Services who support, advise and signpost sufferers, carers and loved ones.

To Faye, Katy and Fiona, your support and thoughtfulness have been valuable. It has been comforting to know that you are thinking of us. I wish you all the very best in your journeys. And not forgetting Angela and members (eating disorder support group), thank you for always making me feel so welcome and giving me a safe space to talk.

Finally, to Emmie, my gorgeous scruffy dog. I can't miss her out. She wasn't that much help, as she was often asleep, but supported me in her own little way.

About the Author

Emma was born in a small town in South Wales and now lives in Derbyshire with her two children, a cat who likes nothing more than jumping on her laptop when she is working, and her scruffy but adorable dog who melts everyone's heart.

Emma has always been passionate about helping others, which led her into a career in healthcare. Continuously searching for solutions to help her daughter, she has completed several courses and gained a better understanding of mental health illnesses and eating disorders. This ignited a fire in her belly to make a difference and she is now a trained emotional coach and therapist.

By listening to other parents and carers, Emma saw a need to share her story. Writing this book has been a cathartic way to help her deal with her daughter developing anorexia and she hopes that it will offer support to others on the same path.

Emma admits to being a fan of Welsh rugby and loves watching matches with her family, particularly if they win. When she is not writing or supporting her daughter, she enjoys spending time outdoors, walking her dog and taking photographs.